BELOVED,
I CAN SHOW YOU
HEAVEN

BELOVED, I CAN SHOW YOU HEAVEN

A True Story of Life After
Death Communication
Between Soulmates

Jennifer Angelee

Copyright © 2020 Jennifer Angelee

All rights reserved. No part of this book may be used or reproduced by any means, graphic, electronic, or mechanical, including photocopying, recording, taping or by any information storage retrieval system without the written permission of the author except in the case of brief quotations embodied in critical articles and reviews.

The author has tried to recreate events, locales, and conversations from the memories of them. In order to maintain their anonymity in some instances, the author has changed the names of individuals, places, identifying characteristics and details of physical properties and residences.

Contact the author at jenniferangelee.com

Cover design by Pagatana Designs—pagatana.com

Cover image: Shutterstock.com

Other books by Jennifer Angelee:
Stairway to Heaven
Miracles of Love, Faith and Hope
I Can Show You Heaven
Angel Bumps

ISBN
978-1-7774760-0-7 (paperback)
978-1-7774760-1-4 (ebook)

This book is dedicated to my dear husband and soulmate, Joe. Joe, I promise you that I will go on without you. I will have courage that will make you smile down from heaven with pride. I will care for our children with all our love, and when this life is over, I will run into your arms and want to start all over again with you.

~ A Note About Suicide ~

Suicide is Never the Answer

Although there is beauty in this story, it is not something I would ever choose for my life or my children's life. I miss the physical presence of my husband everyday, every moment, every hour. I know it was not his intention to die and to leave his family mourning a tragic loss. I never want anyone to suffer the pain and sadness my children and I have endured.

Suicide is never the answer. I believe that anyone that is open to it can heal their lives.

Please, if you are thinking about suicide, seek help and call your local crisis or distress line or emergency services. There are many more resources available online. Suicide is never the answer. It is not your time. Life is precious and you don't need to rush to the finish line.

Table of Contents

Preface xi
Introduction xiii

Chapter 1:   A Love in Bloom 1
Chapter 2:   Cut by the Thorns of Love 5
Chapter 3:   A Rose Picked for the Heavenly Garden 13
Chapter 4:   A Fallen Angel 18
Chapter 5:   Rose Petals and Baby's Breath 22
Chapter 6:   In Search of My Rose 29
Chapter 7:   The Sharpest Thorns 40
Chapter 8:   Soft Petals and Angel Wings 81
Chapter 9:   The Thorn and the Roses 96
Chapter 10: A Fallen Rose's Thorns Remain 106
Chapter 11: Forgiveness is the Fragrance of the Rose 126
Chapter 12: In the Arms of the Angels 136
Chapter 13: Rose Petals from Heaven 140
Chapter 14: Rose Petals Drop on Fallen Snow 150
Chapter 15: My Ascended Beloved 154
Chapter 16: Heaven and Hope 172
Chapter 17: On the Stairway to Heaven 175
Chapter 18: Messages from My Beloved 182
Chapter 19: When Tomorrow Starts Without You 187
Chapter 20: Dreams of My Beloved 210

Epilogue	219
Afterword	221
References	225
About the Author	227

Preface

My world was torn apart the day my husband and father of my children died by suicide May 13, 2015. My husband Joe was 44 years old and our three living children were 17, 12, and 8. We had been together for twenty-five years and we fell madly in love when I was only eighteen years old. He was my rock, my strength and the love of my life.

Joe was an incredible light in this world. His beautiful smile could lift anyone's spirit, but being married to him was the most wonderful gift. He was a devoted husband and heroic father, giving our son Nicholas a life-saving kidney the summer of 2012 after a decade of helping to manage our son's kidney disease.

For anyone who knew Joe, he was the last person they would suspect of taking his own life. Joe was never diagnosed with mental illness, not even depression. Some would call Joe the strong, silent type who kept his deepest feelings to himself. I was blessed to be the closest one in the world to him, and of course, this makes grieving him the greatest burden.

In January 1999, Joe and I lost our second child, Joseph. He was stillborn and passed away from the same exceedingly rare disease as our oldest child. As difficult as that loss was for me, Joe never really got over the tremendous loss of this very special soul. I know that they are together in heaven.

After Joe's sudden and seemingly senseless death, I was heartbroken. In desperation, I did whatever I could to heal so that my children and I could go on. I also sought answers from Joe on the other side, and many times Joe found me from heaven without my searching.

I met many Mediums on my grieving journey, and even became a channel and a Medium myself for Joe to communicate through. I want to take this opportunity to thank the Mediums in this book for their contributions that made *Beloved, I Can Show You Heaven* possible. Each one of you is incredibly special to me and I am forever grateful for your gracious words that carried me through my darkest hours. Each of you is spiritually gifted and a blessing that brings a little heaven to Earth.

There are many profound mediumship readings in the pages of this book. Readings that not only talk about my relationship with my husband, but readings that contain wisdom for living a life on earth where we don't have to die to experience heaven.

Joe became a self-proclaimed guardian angel and spirit guide for me, teaching me about heaven and the other side. But most of all, Joe, as my soulmate, teaches me about the power of love and what it can do.

Follow me as I take you on a journey of love, heartache, and heaven, as my Beloved shows us that heaven is the divine love that we have for one another.

Introduction

"Love liberates, it doesn't bind. It loves you if you're in China, it loves you if you're across town. I love you, I would like to be near you with your arms around me, but that's not possible now." –Maya Angelou

These famous words by American author and poet, Maya Angelou echo in my ears. I heard these words on the Oprah Winfrey Network Super Soul Sunday the Mother's Day morning before Joe's death. On this sunny morning, I sat on my family room sofa with a hot cup of coffee savouring the alone time while Joe and the kids slept late. Joe had worked the night before and he needed rest. When I heard Maya Angelou's words, something powerful inside me stirred, tears poured down my face and I felt like maybe one day, I, like Maya Angelou, would be a great teacher. I thought about how I felt like Joe was holding me back from reaching my potential, how each time I reached for a dream, he wanted to stop me. When Joe woke, I gently tried to discuss how I felt about what I watched, and that in some sense, he needed to liberate me. He got defensive, and the day that I was looking forward to, ended in great pain.

Ironically, I was the one who needed to do the liberating. When Joe died by suicide three days later, I had to learn to let the love of my life go, to liberate his soul and show him and the world that I could achieve dreams on my own. That way, he would be free, but something bigger than who we were in life together happened. As I've heard since I was a young girl, if you love something, you set it free, if it comes back to you, it is true love. Joe came back to me in the most unexpected way. He came back to be my soul guide and to help me live as my true authentic self. In exchange, I completed a life purpose of his, to serve others by his sacrifice, by his example of the unique life he lived.

This book is more than just a tragic love story. It is more than just a story about me, my late husband and our family. My hope is that this book you are reading has brought you here for a higher purpose and to help you be your highest self. Though my beloved died by suicide, it is more than a story about suicide. There is an infinite universal message encrypted on the pages you will be reading; this story is about the eternal love we all share with our Creator and with each other. This is a love that is meant to bring us together as one, rather than separating us from each other.

Much of the information in this book is channelled, meaning that other higher level beings such as my angels and guides, as well as archangels gave ideas and guidance to my higher self to write this book. This came in the form of inspiration when I was living my everyday life. This inspiration and guidance was comfort to the grief I faced each morning I woke after his death. After Joe's death, I was not motivated by the things that got me going previous to his death. Before Joe's passing, I was highly task oriented but unfulfilled, running from the stick, rather than chasing the proverbial carrot. Since a part of me died with Joe, I was living a new life with a fresh perspective. I was, 'smelling the roses' as some might say, but I missed Joe terribly and it was more than that. There was a quantum shift in my energy which caused me to focus on my life as if *I* was already ascended into heaven. I lived each day thinking that the day will come when I'm an old woman and I will also die and go to heaven. I asked myself what was important. My focus and priorities changed. I wanted the life I lived to be so good, that when I died, I would leave the world a better place by making positive changes within me.

So I began to live each day doing something I would otherwise regret not having done when I die. This involved publishing my first book *Miracles of Love, Faith and Hope*, a book that took me almost a decade to write. I also delved into the spiritual world and became trained as a Reiki Practitioner, a Certified Medium, and Angel Guidance and Healing Practitioner. I noticed that my soul was ascending while in my physical body and my spiritual healing and psychic abilities became enhanced. I then wrote *Stairway to Heaven, A Step by Step Guide to Ascension Healing on Earth,* as a means of teaching others how to ascend their energetic frequency, the way I had done.

With this training and enhanced clairvoyant abilities, I had an idea to start my own healing modalities under a business name inspired by my husband called *The Healing Temple*, named after what he called the beautiful structure he built in our backyard before he gave our son his kidney. He said, "This is *The Healing Temple* for my family to heal in."

I was also working on concepts for my own spiritual psychotherapy modality and getting my first children's book, *Angel Bumps* published. Of course, there was writing this book also. For the first months I watched the story in these pages unfold, writing only jot notes not to forget the big ideas. I saved all of my audio mediumship readings on my iPhone, to be transcribed at a later date.

I felt compelled to write as part of my healing; a cathartic way to get it all out so I could get all the thoughts that swim in my mind out on paper. That way I was not stuck in a revolving door that encircled the past. My soul yearned to be free as I felt it expanding into the consciousness of Source, our Divine Creator, where my beloved is with God.

I know that all of what I just described sounds like quite the bucket list for a grieving young widow with three kids to support. It is, but that's one of the reasons I had for writing this book. I wanted to be a living example of living life as your highest and most actualized self, even in the face of adversity or tragedy.

Joe was never diagnosed or treated for any form of mental illness, nor was he seeing his doctor. I soon became an amateur forensic psychologist extraordinaire. Despite my effort, I realized how limited the psychiatric and psychological community are in their suicide knowledge, understanding and resources. This motivated me to dig deeper into not only the reasons for my husband's death, but I recognized the importance of educating others on suicide.

Within the few days before my husband's death, I witnessed a sudden decline in the man that I was married to. He was depleted physically, mentally and emotionally. I felt he became victim to overwork and had lost awareness of himself and those closest to him. I know that Joe was 'impaired' during the act of his suicide and did not intend to die. He was impaired from lack of sleep as he had been on night shift for several consecutives months and refused to advocate for himself. The night before

Joe's death, I knew he needed to take a long sabbatical from work and see our family doctor. But we had an argument and I pleaded with him not to go into work that night when Joe said he was so tired that he could kill himself.

I tried to logically tell him to go to bed and sleep at dinner time but he lost his temper. Little did I know that these outbursts were a symptom of a much deeper issue manifesting as depression. I thought I was just making him angry, that there was something wrong with me because I could not please my husband. When I drove away to do an errand that night, I remember telling myself clearly that the solution to Joe's problem was for him to take the summer off. I knew that what I had to do was to take this sick man into the doctor to secure time off of work, with or without pay. After all, we had one month until we were mortgage and debt free, we had worked hard and we could finally afford it because I was now working full-time since our son's recovery from his kidney transplant from Joe.

Joe's death brought strain to many of my relationships with our family members. Supporting a young widow whose husband died by suicide is not something that most people are comfortable with. Most people in my life did not have the emotional, mental or spiritual capacity to support me in the way that I needed. One person said I was the cause of Joe's decision to take his own life. I am only mentioning this because I feel it is crucial to bring awareness to the issue of blame in suicide. Of course, at first I blamed myself also. I think that guilt is a natural part of grieving the suicide of someone close to you. Guilt made mourning Joe extraordinarily difficult and many times it caused me to feel like I was hanging onto my own life by my fingernails. Knowing how my children needed me to guide and raise them forced me to keep going. I knew that if they didn't have me, they would be forever broken.

Bringing awareness to issues around suicide and suicide grief is crucial. Media sometimes depicts an acceptance of suicide and the blame of the act on anyone other than the one who died by it. In this book, I intensely investigate the reasons my husband was lead to do what he did.

I was often asked by people why my husband took his life. This question made me uncomfortable because if someone asks this they are under the assumption that perhaps there is an acceptable reason, either within the person's psyche or in their external life. I want people to understand that my husband made an irreversible poor choice to do what he did. In the readings it is revealed that my husband accepts responsibility for his actions in his physical life. He recognizes his shortfalls in life and that he could overcome problems in his life. He discusses these issues in the mediumship readings in this book.

Many of us face extraordinarily difficult life challenges without emotional support. Joel Osteen, a popular young preacher on Sunday morning T.V. was a comfort for me. I have never cared for evangelical preachers, but Joel is so genuine, I can see how God has put favour on his life to help others. Before each episode I wondered what his topic was going to be and I was always surprised how fitting it is for where I was in my life. One thing Joel helped me remember is that God puts people in your life who are your enemies and your naysayers. You may not realize it, but they are put there to bring your dreams about, to stir you up inside, so you don't become complacent. Negative people are there to set you up for success. Everybody knows the feeling that makes you want something even more when someone is against you. I have certainly had my share of these negative people, naysayers and betrayers since Joe's death, and Joel's reminder has helped me on my journey of grief.

More importantly, different types of people are all part of living an earthly life. One need only look at Jesus' life for examples of betrayers and doubters, from Judas to Thomas, but we are here to overcome all of this, to be honest and true to ourselves and to love one another.

Each day after Joe's death I worked just a little towards my hopes for a new future, I refused to think, 'When this happens, then I will do that', because when you say 'someday', that 'someday' never comes, and you lead a life of regret. I know because that was me for the first forty-two years of my life. When Joe died I was left holding the bag of tremendous responsibility and I think of the life I could have had with my beloved husband. He threw my 'someday' out the window, a 'someday' which had him and I painted all over it. My canvas of life faded to black while my heart was still beating in my chest.

I sometimes wonder if Joe lived the life of his dreams, or if he even had dreams at all. I don't know and it pains me to think he could have had it all. I will probably never know if it was Joe's destiny to die at the age of 44. If only Joe had taken some risks or asked for help then maybe he would still be alive and happy today. Each day I wondered about this.

Unfortunately I have no power to change this physical death. All I know is that for me, one door slammed shut in my face and instead of choosing to wallow in self-pity, I walked through the door that swung wide. The fork in the road was no longer a fork-shape but became an arrow, pointing only one way – up!

This is a story of my healing journey, not just healing from the worst grief I have ever felt in my life, the most miserable stuff anyone could deal with, but healing everything about me. Please don't get me wrong, I will never, ever 'get over it', and even if I did, that is not the point because grief changes you, but that hole in your heart can become a catalyst in becoming the 'whole' you. Becoming your true authentic self in one lifetime is a journey of death and re-birth.

I recently did a quiz online to see what my totem animal is. Unsurprisingly, I was a butterfly which has been a recurring theme in my life. I feel the metamorphosis within me. It's like the first half of my life I was a hungry caterpillar, eating all the leaves to fatten up for a big change. I am at last emerging from my dark cocoon to spread my wings.

I hope that this book answers some important questions about what happens to a suicide in death and what it is like in heaven. In religion and society there are preconceived notions about the afterlife when a suicide takes place. Given my intimate experience with suicide death and the afterlife, I want to pierce the bubble of these negative perceptions, and bring forth clarity and light to the understanding of this very prominent issue of suicide in our modern world.

When my husband was alive, I thought I knew his life story. But when he died, I began to channel his soul story, about his life. That's when things began to make more sense to me. His life became a wonderful example for me and gave me more clarity about life and its meaning.

A lot of healing took place for both of us, despite the fact that Joe was in heaven. I believe that what we don't get on the physical plane, our almighty Creator gives us a chance to learn in heaven.

Joe and I were partners in every sense of the word. In life, he was good at everything that I was not, and vice versa. We did everything together and we were inseparable. I believe that in life, Joe tried to help me in any and every way he could. He adored me and protected me. It was so difficult to learn to live without his physical presence. Soon, however, Joe became one of my soul guides. In this sense, we are still partners and soulmates. As painful as it is this way, he is my soulmate in an even larger sense. Our souls are still infinitely connected as I finish my incarnation with Joe in the spiritual form.

At the end of writing this book, I came back to the realization that Joe and I were remarkably similar in our thoughts, beliefs and experiences. I too experienced at times what it was like to be emotionally fragile, but I was more conscious and aware of myself than Joe was. I know that life is a precious gift and that we are co-creators of our destiny.

Survivor's guilt plagued me. If it were not for our children in those early days of grief, I would have wanted to join my Beloved on the other side. However I believe it is my destiny to live on and continue to evolve in this lifetime. I will continue to honour my husband's memory and his continued purpose from the other side.

Oftentimes I wondered where Joe was, and what he was doing. I wondered if he even cared about me at all. I wondered why he didn't visit me in my dreams the night before, and why things went wrong sometimes.

I am however, tremendously blessed to receive beautiful messages from heaven from my Beloved. He showed me that heaven is the place of undying love, where we are one with our Source and our Creator. Heaven is a place where we are free of our ego consciousness, and we are free of all negativity. When we die, *Love* is the only thing we take with us and it is magnified in the glory of universal consciousness of our loving God, Creator and Source of all that is.

Please allow me to take you on this journey of eternal love, a journey to Heaven and Source through the soul of one man. Welcome to this journey with my Beloved as the guide of this spiritual quest into an afterlife experience as my loving partner and soul mate, Joe.

Chapter 1

A Love in Bloom

"We delight in the beauty of the butterfly, but rarely admit the changes it goes through to achieve its beauty." –Maya Angelou

I never thought much of the concept of soulmates until my husband died by suicide on May 13, 2015. It was as if my heart was ripped from my chest and a gaping, hollow wound filled the space where my heart seemed to beat in unison with his. He left me with no explanation and three young, beautiful children. He was only 44 years old. I was 42.

We fell madly in love when I was 18 years old and in my last year of high school. It was March 1991. A mutual friend felt we were perfect for each other. She described him as smart, ambitious and really cute, a go-getter like me. When we met that late winter day at her house I had just come from skating. I was doing my teaching co-op for high school and felt I needed some practice before taking my classes skating that week.

He was 20 years old. He had long, curly dark hair, light brown eyes and a beautiful smile with perfect white teeth and deep red, supple lips that were full in the middle and thin at the corner of his grin. He was six foot tall and had a slim, muscular build.

This was not the first time our paths had crossed. Early on in our relationship we recalled our experiences from when we had attended the same Catholic high school together. He told me how he vividly remembered me, my aqua green eyes and how I looked in my school girl uniform and kilt. He said I was the most beautiful thing he had ever seen. He said I was like a tall, slender child and even remembered my knees, the small bit of flesh between my tall grey socks and my long, modest kilt. He said he remembered exactly where my locker was and each day he tried to get the nerve to talk to me, but could not.

I have one strange memory of him when we were in grade nine. I was walking out of the cafeteria at lunch in the opposite direction of him. He had girls on each side of him and he had a silly grin on his face. I glanced in his direction and took notice of this cute boy in an atypical version of the Catholic school boy ensemble. He was tall, slender, but not my type at all. He had a punky, new wave style, and curly, slicked back hair with frosted blonde tips, black eyeliner, pointy black leather shoes and he had tapered uniform pants around his ankles. He was the 80's version of a new wave James Dean. When he walked past, I was astonished by how I was overcome with jealousy, an emotion foreign to me. I wondered what and who I was jealous of, for I had not known him or the girls he was with.

On our first date four years later, I told him of my ambitions to go to University the upcoming September and that I wanted to travel abroad and study people of indigenous cultures. I was to be a career woman and was not going to be tied down in a relationship or have anyone stop me. I had been hurt before and this time I thought it best to draw the line in the sand before having my heart broken again. Joe was immediately disappointed by the idea that I was leaving our home town to pursue my education.

Our second date was most memorable. I remember sitting in the movie theatre and holding his hand. It was as if a current of electricity ran between our hands. I have never felt such magic in all of my life. After the movie we headed to a club across the street from the local college and saw a Van Halen cover band. We danced and the heat between us was palpable. After the concert, we returned to his large, black, Chevy Scottsdale pick-up truck. It had a bench seat and the loud roar of an old muffler. It was ruggedly sexy like Joe and he pulled me close to his side as he drove me home.

When we arrived at my home, he finally kissed me. It was the most tender, loving kiss in the world and I wanted it to last forever. I could not sleep that night. I was falling in love against my will and visions of him danced in my head as if I was a child awaiting Christmas morning.

We spent every moment we could of our busy lives together. He was in college and both of us had part-time jobs. When we weren't together, all we thought about was each other. When I flew to California to see my sister that March Break, only days after knowing him, he was all I could think about. He surprised me at the airport on my return home to Toronto with flowers.

He was the most romantic boyfriend any girl could ever ask for. That Easter, my Mom invited him for our large family dinner. I remember him picking me up for church with a stuffed white Easter bunny with glasses. He came to the door with a single pink rose and moved the bunny forward and said "Happy Easter Four Eyes". I wore glasses for near-sightedness and he lovingly teased me.

Each date he brought me a single rose wrapped beautifully in babies breath from a local florist near his home. As I continued on through five years of University, he would pick me up every weekend and each time he showed up with these same beautiful flowers. Each time I answered the door, we would embrace. The flowers were never as good as breathing in the scent of him at the base of his neck after a long week of study. He was such a beautiful light of energy. I was instantly uplifted in his presence and each time I held him, I did not want to let go.

Occasionally, there was a dark side to him that became absent and withdrawn. A part of him that would not let me in and it frustrated me to no end. He would just shut down and become emotionless. I remembered leaving his house in anger and walking home during our first fight. I don't remember any issue; I just remember that familiar feeling of suddenly being shut out and him not being able to communicate with me or express emotion.

He was incredibly stubborn and had extraordinary willpower. Somehow, we got through those dark moments and moved forward as if they had never happened at all.

Joe proposed to me just after Christmas 1994 on the beach at sunset in Carmel, California when I was in my final year of my undergraduate degree. We began making wedding plans the following winter when I was in Teacher's College and we married that summer in August, 1996.

To everyone, he was the perfect, adoring husband. We worked hard and that autumn we purchased our first house, a new construction for the following year. We were saving for a down payment and I became pregnant in February of 1997 with our son. I was only 24 years old but I felt this deep seated fear that I was going to lose Joe early on. I perpetually worried about his safety. His job had an element of risk and Joe was fearless. He used to work extreme outdoor heights as an iron worker and would walk steel beams without proper harnessing. He was still working long hours with heights under extreme conditions.

A couple days after our wedding, we had our first married fight. I witnessed Joe feeling emotionally hopeless and this was the first time he threatened to kill himself. He scared me as he charged out of the house and then sat alone outside. I knew so little what to say, what to do.

Nevertheless, Joe and I went on to share an incredible life together. The children we brought into this world together are testament to our love. When Nicholas was born in early October 1997, we had just moved into our new home. Nicholas was a joy to us, and I was soon pregnant again with Joseph.

In January 1999, when I was only seven months pregnant, we lost Joseph. Having a stillborn son was heartbreaking for both of us, but Joe never completely came to terms with Joseph's absence in our lives.

Our son Nicholas became extremely ill with an undiagnosed condition and kidney disease in June 2002, just weeks after I became pregnant with our daughter, Faith who was born January 2003. When our beloved Faith was a baby, Joe almost donated his kidney to Nicholas but Nicholas miraculously recovered enough not to need it at that time.

In October 2006, Joe and I brought our youngest child Hope into the world and felt that our family was complete. In the summer of 2008 Joe and our young family moved into a larger four bedroom home with a lot big enough to hold our dream pool, and with space for our growing family to play in.

Our life together was far from easy, but the remarkable thing is that through all the challenges of loss, illness, hard work, and conflict, Joe and I never fell out of love with one another. Joe and I always shared a passion for each other that was rare and intense, not to mention irreplaceable.

The love we shared was full of compassion and forgiveness. There is no question in my mind that we were, and still are divine soulmates. Our love for each other is romantic as a red rose, as deep as the ocean, as vast as the universe, and as immortal as God.

Chapter 2

Cut by the Thorns of Love

"And now my bitter hands cradle broken glass of what was everything." ~ Pearl Jam

May 13, 2015 was the beginning of my fortunate life turning into a nightmare. The rug was pulled out from under me and my world was turned upside down. Joe hung himself in the fruit cellar in the basement of our home. I was home from work and ill that weekday morning. I had slept in. When I awoke I felt weak and called for Joe. My throat felt closed and I barely had the energy to call him. I reached for the phone and called his cell, expecting he could not hear my voice. I phoned his cell again but the recording from the phone company said, "The person you are trying to reach is not answering."

This was not unusual and so I dragged myself from bed with legs as heavy as lead and walked downstairs to the basement. I headed to his workshop in the fruit cellar and opened the door, the light was off and I turned around and walked upstairs to the garage through the main floor mud room entrance. He was not there. I checked through the front living room window and saw his van in the driveway. This puzzled me as he did not seem to be home. Next, I checked the yard, though I had not heard him doing any work that morning. The pool house and shed doors were closed and from the family room window at the back of the house, I could see there was nobody inside. Each time I checked I seemed to move more slowly and heavily than ever until all I could do was manage to take the phone to the sofa and call my son on his cell phone at school. When he answered I asked him if he knew where Dad was because I knew he had seen him before school that morning. He said he did not know where he is and asked me if I wanted him to come home. I said *no,* and thought that my husband was either hiding from me or playing some kind of cruel game. It was unlike him to have gone for a walk in the daytime and my son returned my call. My son insisted on coming home.

Time sped up and before I knew it my son was home and marched into the basement. I heard our son talking and for an instant I felt relief that he had found his Dad hiding in the work shop in the fruit cellar and was arguing with his father; trying to reason with him like he had a few days before. Joe had been completely unreasonable the days before and I thought that he must have withdrawn and was in the fruit cellar hiding from me. I had thought that when I checked the room moments earlier that he was actually there, but I did not see him because I did not look further behind the door that opened into the narrow room.

Apprehensively I walked toward the front hall of the house confused, legs still heavy as lead. I stopped at the top of the stairs and asked Nicholas what was going on. I called "Nicholas, what's going on? Nick what's happening?"

Nicholas bravely replied, "Mom, don't come down here! Just unlock the front door!" I heard his voice of authority speaking to someone. Apprehensively I walked toward the front door confused but knowing I needed to follow this instruction. Once again, Nicholas shouted up to me not to come downstairs. Just as I unlocked the door, a storm of uniformed officers and attendants came through the front door and into my basement.

Everything happened so fast, the events blurred. I remember phoning my parents home and saying to my Dad that "Joe had hung himself" in a desperate voice. Before I knew it, my Dad, Joe's Mom and several family members were at my house. I was in complete shock. My beloved husband and father of my children was pronounced dead. My son begged them to continue CPR. He yelled at the officers to keep trying, but it was too late. My Joe was gone and my children lost their Dad. I cried, "He was the best husband and Dad in the world" as if Joe could hear me. I just wanted him to know how much we loved him, because I felt his presence near me in the house. Those words were intended for Joe and nobody else.

Strangely as I was frozen in fear sitting on the living room sofa at the front of our home, a police officer was kneeling and talking to me, breaking the terrible news to me. I cannot remember the words she said or what she looked like, but as I stared past her in frozen shock, I saw my beloved kneeling down by the glass coffee table in front of me. It was as if he was there, feeling horrible about the news I was getting and his spirit was trying to comfort me. My eyes were wide open and what I saw of him was the spiritual image of exactly what he looked like, and exactly what he would have done had he been there.

Months later I came to the realization that the heaviness in my legs was clearly Joe's spirit attaching to me. It was as if Joe was hanging onto me, trying to slow me down; he didn't want me to find him and he was clinging to my body, hanging onto what he was most afraid to lose once he passed to the other side. I also believe that he did not want me to find him. He knew how that would scar my mind forever and in hindsight I don't know how I would have reacted if I had been the one to find him.

Regrettably, I never did go downstairs to say goodbye. I never had the strength and I did not want to remember Joe that way. The devastation was real in my mind. I could not witness the physical demise of the man whose warm embrace was the strength that held me up in life.

My world was torn apart and nothing would ever be the same again. The weeks following were the most dreadful weeks of my life. I felt abandoned and alone. I had lost my life partner, my best friend, my lover. Together for over 24 years, Joe was my past, present and future. The beautiful home we created together was a painful reminder of the arduous work and planning we had done. It was all painful and meaningless without him.

I only survived those weeks because of my children and my desire to protect them from the atrocity we were facing. Even having survived the death of a child and the possible mortality of our son Nicholas to his exceedingly rare illness, these were the darkest days of my life.

I agonized to make sense of the senseless. I immediately blamed myself and beat myself up from the inside. I hated myself and felt like dying. Each time I came to the realization that Joe was gone, I would vomit. I dropped 15 pounds in two weeks. The heavy, empty feeling in my heart made everyday tasks seem impossible. My knees knocked in fear and I was terrified of how to do anything without Joe. Still, I pulled myself forward for my three incredible children.

It's so painful to go into the details of the funeral but what I can say is that Joe was loved. Swarms of people came to send their condolences. The visitations were full of many people whose lives were touched by Joe and this was the first time I met them. Friends and neighbours from long past came, and I felt it was like meeting everyone I had ever known before.

After the funeral, the reality of living a life without Joe hit. My life seemed it could never bring me joy and meaning again. Each thing I worked for was for a future with my immaculate partner. He was the most attractive, intelligent, loveable man I'd ever known, and I had always overlooked his dark side that he so desperately kept to himself. All his positive qualities overcame his negative ones and I would not trade having him around for anything in the world. I would never have left him no matter how he disappointed me. I would never have given up on our love, no matter how difficult he was.

I had thought the way to overcome relationship problems was not to work on the other person, but to work on your self. So that's what I tried to do before Joe's death. I worked on what made me feel happy and successful, though I was never truly fulfilled, perhaps because where Joe was concerned, the dots did not connect. It seemed that at my best, Joe would nosedive and seemingly sabotage what I had worked for. Don't get me wrong, it was so subtle and probably unintentional, the way he would betray my carefully laid plans, that it was difficult to accuse him of hurting me. Deep down inside I blamed myself for every mishap. I blamed my impatience and my sharp tongue, those were excellent scapegoats for someone who wanted to play the victim role. Joe oscillated between playing the victim and the hero, cleverly manipulating me with his passive aggressive ways. He was truly unconscious of what he was doing because I know deep down inside, the last thing he wanted to do was hurt me. I was his beloved. To him, I was the sun, the moon and the stars.

We worked on many home improvement projects together. No matter what I did, I always found a way to include him. Even at work, he was always happy to help me out with handy little favours wherever he could. Sometimes, however, he seemed to sabotage me at the best of times. His outbursts happened when I was happy and working independently on my own things. He would become quiet and withdrawn and retaliate when I gently provoked him to open up in pure frustration. He would become furious for a range of my reactions to his moods. I was never subservient to his moods but had grown used to his ups and downs. I felt guilty for many things as I could be an extraordinarily demanding wife. Mostly, he never minded, but without my requests and reminders, I felt that he would take no initiative or remember anything that needed to be done. He was a tasks person, liked routine and was stubborn and set in his ways. I focussed on order and creativity, always overseeing the kids and all the activity in our busy home to exhaustion.

Just three days before Joe's death, we were invited to one of Joe's family members on Mother's Day. We were scheduled to be there at noon for lunch. At 11:45 a.m. the phone rang while I was making his mother's gift and was running behind. Joe answered and he was told they were going to eat without us. Joe did not explain why we were late; we were not careless, but carefully making gifts for our mother's. When he hung up the phone, I asked him why he made us look bad, but Joe was clearly hurt and disappointed. This led us to an argument and I began to feel the dark energy hang above my head like a thick, black storm cloud. As I gently tried to challenge his defensive behaviour, Joe retaliated, jumping out of his seat with widened eyes, "Well if you feel that way about me, I'm just going to kill myself!"

In pure frustration, trying to cool the situation like putting a blanket on a fire of rage, I stood, grabbed his face in my palms, looked him in his eyes, and stated, "Stop saying that!!"

As I starred into his eyes, they met mine with the cold stare of an angry demon. I was looking at him squarely in the eye. My beloved was not there; in his place was a cold monster that looked at me without a care. I held his large head in my small hands, not knowing what to do next. We had a stare down, and I asked Joe to sit down on the sofa across from me to talk.

As I sat across from him, I began to feel very strange. I told Joe I felt that there was literally a black cloud over my head. I told him I felt fuzzy in the head, like something really bad was happening or was about to happen. I told him, "Please, you don't understand. It feels so dreadful. I feel a black cloud over us. I have a bad feeling something terrible is going to happen." I felt that somehow he had the power to fix it much like he fixed everything else. But he seemed so unwilling to help and to change his dreadfully stubborn mood despite my suffering. He coldly looked at me without a word, and so I repeated hoping he would give me comfort to make the horrible feeling go away.

The time seemed to warp for us and eventually sped forward as we debated about the value of our lives. I told him I could never leave our children, and that if anything ever happened to me, Hope would be lost without me. I told him our lives would be extremely difficult without him, and that financially we would be devastated without his income to support us. Joe had threatened to kill himself so many times in a fit of rage that I never truly believed our long life together was coming to an end. Joe was the strong one that I looked up to. Though I often challenged him, I also feared him knowing the power that lay dormant like a sleeping volcano, capable of erupting with any pressure.

In hindsight, I think how stupid could I be to ignore his threats and not get him help. I perhaps should have known better. Instead I empathically took on his feelings as my own. My thinking was not clear, I was not objective. Joe and I were so close that I could not separate my consciousness from his. I think if I had seen this behaviour in anyone else, I would have been alarmed enough to get appropriate help. I just kept trying to get him to change his behaviour, trying to control the situation until it dissipated into normal, everyday routine.

It was too late to go to his family's, so we tried to salvage the day and go to mine. Joe drove the car and I was nervous about his driving. He was angry at me for being nervous and it was a cold battle all the way there as we tried not to argue in front of the kids. While there, Joe was sullen and withdrawn, socializing little with my family.

When we left, he got in the van and left without thanking the host, or saying goodbye. As soon as I mentioned this, he turned argumentative and defensive. He never considered it was Mother's Day, hadn't given me a card or a gift, or even wished me Happy Mother's Day. I was crushed. Arguing was futile. I gave up trying and felt hopeless about us. Later at bedtime, I came downstairs to find a Mother's Day Card left on the kitchen table. It was as basic as basic could be. I was hurt that he waited to the very end of the day to give it to me and hadn't even had the courage to give it to me but left it laying around for me to find, whenever. The lack of compassion and effort made me hurt and frustrated. I walked away crying hoping he would follow. He did not. I took the cards my children gave me, placed them on my night table and I cried myself to sleep. He walked into my room and witnessed my pain and offered me no consolation.

This was unusual for me but I was feeling I was always pushing water uphill. The days before Joe's death, he did not seem to care about anything, especially me. I was hurt by his callousness and retreated from the cycle of fighting him. He was not himself and for a brief moment I gave up hoping that when he saw how he had hurt me, he would at last change once and for all. This time I was not going to tell him when and how to make it up to me.

The following day was Monday and Joe was quiet and tired and spoke few words to me. I wanted to make up with him and I wanted things to be calm and peaceful. I would not broach the subjects brought up on the Sunday, for fear of another showdown. Joe was tired and despondent but eventually he seemed to be coming around but remained quiet in the coming hours. He asked me if I wanted him to go to my hospital appointment out of town. I told him that I would like to be with him, but it wasn't necessary and suggested he could stay home and sleep as he had been on the night shift. He accompanied me to the hospital and said very little.

The Tuesday night before Joe's death, I sadly never got a chance to tell Joe to take a medical leave to relieve his anxiety and burnout. Instead, conflict erupted and I became upset. I went to my bathroom to hide away and realized that the way I had been feeling the months before was not me, but I was picking up on Joe's energy. Joe followed me and I declared that all along my physical symptoms were related to him. In recognizing the truth in what I said in tears and tremendous upset, Joe dropped to his knees and told me he was sorry.

I had forgiven Joe so many other times, and he never changed or moved any situation forward. Exasperated by years of being the victim to Joe's dark moods, I rejected his apologies. I was so devastated by what he had put me through so many times in our lives together, I couldn't bring myself to forgive him. I felt that my tough love was the only thing that could bring this incredibly stubborn man's behaviour in check. We had argued into many nights and days, while he never understood how desperate I felt in our relationship without my emotional needs being met. I knew I was loved, even adored, but in Joe's love there was now only hurt. I couldn't hold on when all I could do was crawl, and didn't have the strength to stand alone.

I repeatedly analyzed the events of those days and the words said, and asked myself two questions that balance themselves in an agonizing tug of war: "What could I have done and said?" and "How could he?"

Chapter 3

A Rose Picked for the Heavenly Garden

"There is a crack in everything that is how the light gets through." -Leonard Cohen

Joe's death felt like an axe has fallen from the sky and had separated everything that was familiar to me. This included family relationships which became strained and I knew that some jumped to assumptions about why Joe took his life. At times I felt blamed and shunned. This was like insulting a wounded soldier in battle but in my bewilderment I was determined to learn the truth.

Love finds a way and I got answers that no one else could. Joe was determined to let me know the truth as well, and as heartbreaking as it was, the not knowing was worse. Two days after his death, I returned home from the funeral home. With all the chaos, the kids and I never had a chance to even begin mourning. When I came home that afternoon, I knew I needed to be there for my children, they too had been so strong, and needed to express their loss. I remember we were laying on the bed in Nicholas' room, Faith on my left, Nicholas on my right. They were sobbing and I knew I had to be the presence and strength they needed. The pain in the space I held for them was so unbearable that I wanted to squirm out of my skin, jump off the bed and run. I held them mentally, emotionally and physically as my poor babies had to deal with an unthinkable loss inflicted on their lives. I thought the ache would never subside when suddenly there was a shift in energy that Joe was releasing through our daughter Faith.

Faith began to channel her Daddy. Our sobs quieted and we listened with still intent to the beautiful things that our beloved was telling Faith. At first Faith was sobbing as she talked about the special things about her Dad; how he would text her everyday on the school bus on her way home from school, how he would always say 'Faith is the only one who eats all her snacks', and how she would eat all her grapes but always leave just one for him to eat after school when he emptied her lunch bag and containers. He was that 'hands on' Dad, clearly there was an incredibly special bond between the two of them, and she was telling me things I had never realized were their special ritual. I felt the loss of a very special Dad that I would never be able to replace.

Faith's fond memories turned into her telling us what her Daddy was telling her at that exact moment. She said, "Daddy said that he will be riding the bus to school with me everyday. He will be sitting on my left side." Then Faith began to tell us all the things he had been doing in heaven already. "He said that he is with all his family there, and he built a house for them".

Faith continued to channel her Dad as she began to give us comforting messages about the future which to us at the time, could not be comprehended without the loving patriarch of our family. She said, "Daddy says Nicholas is going to marry a beautiful girl with long brown hair. He says that Mommy is going to live to be a very old woman…you are going to marry again."

I sensed in an instant a glimmer of hope for what I felt was a daunting and bleak future. Faith continued, "He says he's not going to miss anything. He'll be there when I get married…" Even Nicholas displayed some relief and said, "That's one of the first things I thought, he won't be there to walk the girls done the aisle when they get married."

Bringing my children to see their father's body in the casket was the hardest thing I had to do. I was so apprehensive myself and I wanted to protect my children. Death was not something I wanted these precious young souls to see. Yet it had to be done. A family member came to the funeral home with us to help me watch the kids. I carefully and methodically planned my strategy. First I would go; second, I would bring each child one at a time, oldest to the most precious youngest.

I did not know what to expect and when it was my turn, I slowly walked toward the casket from the middle of the room where the door I entered was. I was gravely disappointed by how Joe looked. He looked sad and angry, frowning. I tried nervously to bring the corner of his lips up but it was not possible. His skin was tough and cold. All I wanted to do was hold his hand, but this was not the hand I had held in marriage. It too was cold and devoid of the warm energy Joe carried in his life. The sting of Joe's death was real and I could not bear to look at his face, or touch the hollow shell of his body. I turned my back to the casket and fell to my knees and sobbed, "I'm sorry Joe!"

In a strange way, I felt his presence in the large, empty room. I needed him to hear my words. Until that moment, I had bottled everything in, trying not to look like a crazy woman. All eyes were on me and I was holding it in to protect my children from being subjected to any more emotional turmoil. After minutes of sobbing, I gained composure and pulled my head off the floor. I got up and walked to the casket and stood behind Joe's head. This way, I could not see his face. I twirled my fingers through his hair and spoke softly to him.

As I brought the kids in, we all held each other close, as we moved in careful procession toward the casket. They had never seen anyone in a casket before and it was so sadly unbelievable it was their Dad. They were so brave as they stood there crying. Faith stood behind Joe's head beside me, twirling his hair as I had done. Again Faith began to channel Joe, "Daddy said he saw all the saints. He met Jesus, Mary, St. Joan of Arc, St. Joseph, St. Ignatius of Loyola, St. James, St. Dominic and St. Andrew."

"Wow," I said, "that's all the saints from the schools we have gone to".

The spiritual journey that began with the loss of our son Joseph gave me the knowledge of heaven that many others did not understand. I had already been spiritually awakened, and so connecting with deceased loved ones was not a foreign concept to me. I remember at the funeral home, the first night of the wake, I was so nervous as the large room of the funeral parlour was near empty with only close family and friends. Joe's family did not speak to me or offer any sort of comfort. They were clearly devastated themselves and the blame everyone placed on me was so palpable, I felt myself wanting to shrink and disappear. I remember collapsing on the sofa and the sinking feeling in my chest. I said to myself, *I don't want to do this,* as I grew more apprehensive of guests arriving. Just after I said that I felt as if Joe was behind my chest, hugging me from behind and holding me up. I took brief notice of it, and just as I did, I felt the ability to rise to the visitors. Before I knew it, the large room of the funeral home was full of people and I was standing steps away from Joe's now closed casket and an enormous line of people, strangers many of them, waiting to greet me. The sorrow and love that they shared gave me strength and I surprised myself again because of the grace and strength I displayed over the pain I felt.

People of all kinds came, many men from Joe's work whom I never met before but heard the occasional name from Joe in casual conversation about work. He worked with a big team of trades people like himself, clearly honest and caring men, but there wasn't much socializing out of work, so they were all new to me. I remember almost nothing of the names and faces that evening, but there is one lady I have such gratitude for and I will never forget. Her name is Cheryl Davidson. Cheryl approached me as this bubbly late 40-something blonde after her husband Bill quietly introduced himself to me as an electrician that Joe worked with.

Cheryl's words stunned me. She introduced herself as a medium explaining what that was, not knowing how familiar I was with the term, having channelled deceased loved ones myself.

She said, "Hi I'm Cheryl. I'm a Medium and I don't know if you know what that is, but I connect with people who have passed in spirit. Your husband wants you to know that he's still madly in love with you and he's standing behind you right now, holding you up. He's hugging you from behind."

She continued in her slight American accent as tears welled in my eyes, "Its okay honey. He says you're really smart, you can do this."

My mouth hung wide but hearing those words were such a relief. Quickly, I pulled her aside needing to talk to her. I knew she had so much to tell me and that was more important than the crowd of people waiting for me. We talked quickly and I felt Cheryl's strength which gave me comfort. Cheryl continued explaining how Joe literally dragged her to the funeral home. She had other plans but had to rearrange them to be there.

Cheryl was so incredibly specific but the next thing she said was enough to seal the deal that she really was connecting with my beloved husband.

"He says your second book is going to be better than your first."

Speechless my mouth hung wide, "Wow" I said. "He was the only one that I told!"

Just two weeks before Joe's death I had a mediumship reading and our son, Joseph, in heaven told me there would be a second book. I went home, told Joe and thought of the name; *Beloved, I Can Show You Heaven!* I didn't really know what it was about but felt that our late son, Joseph would help me write it.

Cheryl continued, telling me that Joe wanted me to know that, '*Third time is a charm*' and he said that, "In our next life together, we would get it right, and live happily ever after." She reiterated how Joe kept saying that he's madly in love with me. There was so much passion in her voice that her presence gave me hope. I am still amazed how Joe brought this complete stranger to both of us, to channel his love for me.

Cheryl was more aware of the wait I was putting my guests through, and handed me her card and told me to call her after the funeral because she had more to tell me and would visit me without charge and fulfil her promise to my husband to connect with me.

Joe's messages were a welcome comfort in the hell we were going through. How this loving soul left us in such a terrible way was such a paradox for the love he had for his family. Whatever caused Joe to abandon us on a physical level, he would not abandon on a spiritual level. I can only imagine that as difficult as it was for us, Joe longed to comfort and hold us as we longed to hold and comfort him.

Chapter 4

A Fallen Angel

"Death leaves a heartache no one can heal, love leaves a memory no one can steal." ~ Irish Headstone

When Joe died, I was not supported in the way that I needed and this was extremely difficult. It was gut-wrenching for me to consider the absence of value I was given as a mother. I felt astounding betrayal and kept my feelings inside both because of the shock I was in and because it was not safe to express my true feelings of profound loss and desperation. My husband had been a protective partner for 25 years sheltering me from the harshness of our worlds. Now it was like my world was erupting like a volcano under the stress, pressure and confusion around his death and he was unable to protect me from the atrocious circumstances.

If Joe were there, he would have protected the children and I courageously. Traumatic death and fear bring out the worst, and I sometimes felt others were draining my energy through my emotional wounds. Suddenly, love had abandoned me, and the only thing surrounding me was fear.

When I returned home the first time after Joe's death, my home felt like a ghost town without the man who made it our home. Realizing that I had no one to turn to, I felt the essence of myself, of who I am. I had not felt that since childhood. Like in childhood, I felt the 'me' I incarnated as, on this planet, and everything on the outside of me was foreign. I was me, and I was a victim. I missed the warmth of union with my soulmate, intertwined, for better or for worse, and in death we were ripped apart.

I was left to make most of the funeral arrangements. No expense was spared for Joe because money was the furthest thing from my mind. I didn't know whether to cremate or bury Joe but I decided on a burial due to his parent's insistence. I didn't even know if I would lose it all and have to sell our home. Life was daunting. Joe's parents never spoke to me at the funeral home or the wakes that were held. To this day, his parents have never reached out to me.

I was as gracious as I could be, and held everything in stoically to be a rock for my children. My children were well supported by their schools, friends and community. It is interesting how those who we least suspect to show up do, and their warmth, understanding and compassion is sometimes greater than those who were the closest part of our lives.

The day of the funeral was a heartbreaking formality. Planning it was equivalent to planning a wedding under extreme stress, grief and anguish. I had not begun the true mourning process and it was up to me to finalize all the details. My older daughter was a rock under the pressure and helped gather and print several photos from our computer. Thankfully my sisters helped shop for funeral dresses for the girls and took care of many details for us.

The last minutes with Joe's body on the day of the funeral were tense as Joe's parent's brought back many distant relatives for their goodbyes. It was supposed to be for close family only – his parents and siblings. Time was tight, and the other guests were waiting 15 minutes away at the church. I snuck back one last time. I needed to be the last one to see Joe. It was my obligation and intention as the closest person in the world to him.

I carefully chose the readings and prayers for his mass. As I walked into the church I grew up in and was married in, I saw the familiar faces of my friends and co-workers on the back left pews. I couldn't help but feel shame despite the fact that they were there to support me. My children and I took our seats at the right front row, alone, just as Joe, Nicholas and I had sat there 16 years earlier at our son Joseph's funeral.

I wanted the mass to honour Joe in our faith. There was no religious judgement for the way that Joe died. The priest was kind and compassionate, despite the negative stereotypes people believe about the church. I want to make note of that because when suicide comes up, a lot of people start pointing their fingers at the Christian faith without knowing the compassion and good that religion provides those who mourn.

The prayer that I chose for Joe's funeral card was the Prayer of St. Francis of Assisi. The one that says:

'Lord, make me an instrument of your peace.
Where there is hatred, let me sow love.
Where there is injury, pardon,
Where there is doubt, faith,
Where there is despair, hope,
Where there is darkness, light,
And where there is sadness, joy.
O Divine Master, grant that I may
Not so much seek to be consoled,
As to console;
To be understood, as to understand;
To be loved, as to love;
For it is in giving that we receive;
It is in pardoning that we are pardoned;
And it is in dying that we are born to eternal life."

In some ways Joe was a master soul and an instrument of peace. Joe lived his life like St. Francis of Assisi. He was a giver, not a taker. He sought understanding of the way the world is, and did not fight to be understood. In many ways, the people closest to him, really didn't know *who* Joe was. Joe tried, in our little world to sow seeds of love, where there was hate and anger. He was my light in the darkness and my joy in the sadness. He didn't seek to receive love as to give love. Even in his darkest hour, he believed he was making a sacrifice for his family, rather than seeking the help he so desperately needed and deserved.

It was though Joe had a disability to love and care for himself. I know as a child, he was not taught to. From a young age, he proved how capable and exceptional he was in other areas. At age 13, he figured out how to wire the basement and became an amateur unlicensed electrician. At age 14, he had his first real job. By grade 11, he was working many hours in construction as an iron worker while going to high school.

From early on in our relationship Joe shared with me that his father had a volatile emotional side. At the same time, Joe was always respectful.

He often felt like an excluded only son. Sadly, his funeral was no exception. I felt that once again, the attention was taken off of Joe as this beautiful soul who was a beautiful person. I did not feel that anyone understood Joe's pain but only their own loss of him. Those closest to him, my children and I were not given the love and compassion for our profound loss of a husband and father. I felt that wasn't honoured or respected. I think that my children must have felt like an apocalypse of their world had taken place, with many adults in their world unable to provide security, reassurance and perspective. I stood strong by them, holding in my emotion, as I held them.

At the cemetery, the guilt I felt magnified as his parent's grief was highly visible and my family stood emotionless. I believe they were confused, in shock and disbelief. I felt their anger and their coldness made me feel blamed for the reason Joe died. I felt harshly and unfairly judged as no one comforted me.

After the service at the cemetery, the kids and I released four white doves to represent the Holy Spirit and the release of Joe's soul from the body. The kids and I released each dove one at a time, and I was last. Each dove flew to the valley where Joe loved to hang out growing up, and I felt a sense of peace within me. For I knew the man that Joe was, and I knew in my heart the place of eternal life, where my beloved would be with our beloved son, Joseph.

Chapter 5

Rose Petals and Baby's Breath

"Your hand fits in mine like it's made just for me, but bear this in mind, it was meant to be. And I'm joining up the dots with the freckles on your cheeks. And it all makes sense to me." ~ One Direction

As seemingly accidental as Joe's suicide was, my investigation into why this happened began with his birth and continued until the hour of his death. There were layers of concentric circles around the reasons why my beloved took his own life. There was nothing Joe or I could do to change what he'd done, but the answers became puzzle pieces that even answered questions about life after death since I was a child.

I was born on a beautiful, warm autumn Tuesday at 6:23 p.m. I was born the baby in a family of eight kids. I was the tie maker, four girls, and four boys. My youngest sibling was almost seven and my oldest was already seventeen. I was an unexpected addition, and the reactions of my siblings to my mother's pregnancy ranged from excitement to disappointment. Nevertheless, my parents welcomed the idea of having new life in the family. My mother went into labour as she raked the leaves of the majestic maple tree in our front yard on a quiet street of ten bungalows in a little suburb outside Toronto, Ontario in 1972. Calmly, she waited for my father to arrive home from work to drive her to the hospital. My Dad dropped her off and was told that I would be awhile so he took my then eight year old brother to coach his hockey practice.

I did not wait for my Dad to return, and though I was told I was nearly two weeks late, my arrival into this world was swift and strong. Throughout my childhood I heard stories around my birth, so much so I recall it now as if I was there. I remember my mother told me about the birth. Compared to her other births, the intensity was great but what was strangest about me was, she said, I did not cry. She said, "You were fine, but your eyes were wide open and you starred at the doctor looking right through him." My mother said she hadn't had a baby that didn't cry when they were born. She said it was the strangest thing, how I stared at everybody's faces.

When the doctor called home to give my father the news, he had not yet returned home. My oldest sister answered the phone and the doctor said, "Tell him it's a girl and she's got the bluest eyes I've ever seen." My sister always went on to tell me the story and that my Dad said the same thing after he saw me.

Doreen Virtue coined the term *Crystal Children* to describe children born with penetrating eyes and Christ conscious souls. Their eyes can lock you in and hypnotize you. They are highly empathic and can sense dishonesty and weak integrity. A friend told me that crystal children are pure, new born souls who often have a challenging life and a difficult life mission. Paradoxically, the great pressure of many past lives crystallizes these souls, like coal turns to diamond after millennium.

Perhaps my coming into this lifetime as a crystal child gave me an understanding of life through my spiritual gifts. All that I was to experience was for the evolution of my soul and to then help others from my experience. I asked this friend how she knew instantly and intuitively that I am a crystal child and she promptly replied, "It's your eyes, I can see it in your eyes".

The spiritual gifts I was born with gave me this ability to empathically feel souls and perceive character. Being highly sensitive however, was a double-edge sword, because many people carry lower energy vibrations. My upbringing was at times emotionally challenging and I repressed this sensitivity growing up.

As a child, I also had a couple of near death experiences but emerged from each one totally unharmed. When I was a baby, I could have choked to death on a small toy from a cereal box. Fortunately, my Dad's emergency first-aid got it out on the way to the hospital. Another time I was walking home with two girlfriends a few blocks from home, when I was hit by a speeding car. I was left unconscious on the ground, but I had no injuries whatsoever. I remember the feeling of fear, running in front of the car and the car gaining on my back and thinking I was about to be hit. I believe I had an out of body experience as I was aware of the things that were happening like my friends running to get help from their moms. The next thing I remember was napping at home and waking up shocked and embarrassed but unscathed. As I grew older this event puzzled me, and I believe I actually fainted before the large, beige 70's sedan hit me. The driver did not stay at the scene, and I believe, in hindsight I was protected by my guardian angel that day because I cannot fathom how I was uninjured.

When I was finally introduced to Joe at the age of eighteen, there was such familiarity with him; it was if my soul had known him all along. I was immediately comfortable around him, and I trusted him. I knew he loved and cared deeply about me from the start. To my surprise, he even expressed his sorrow about an incident in high school when a boyfriend in grade 10 hit me. He told me he desperately wanted to rescue me the day I was hit, but didn't know what to do. He had seen how upset I was in the halls of the high school we attended. Though I never noticed him, he was always watching me knowing there was something incredibly different about me but unable to approach me with his interest.

Each day I wrestle with the circumstances around Joe's death, wondering what I could have done differently, what I said and what I did, wishing I could have changed the outcome. I believe it was destiny that brought us together, and struggle to believe it is destiny that pulled us apart with Joe's departure in the physical. I do believe, however, that Joe fulfilled his life mission to love. I believe that Joe's unique life purpose was not to abandon me, but to love me until it was time for me to learn to love myself.

When Joe and I renewed our Wedding Vows on March 12, 2014, on the beach in Turks and Caicos, we each chose a song for each other. Joe chose *Little Things* by One Direction. I will never forget the true meaning behind the lyrics. Since Joe's death, the song makes better sense as it says, *'If you would only love yourself just as half as much as I love you.'* I feel blessed that I was loved so incredibly by such an amazing person. Ironically, I wish Joe would have loved himself as half as much as I loved him, but I know that in heaven he is complete and wishes he had too.

Incredibly, the evening following Joe's death, Nicholas came downstairs dressed in jeans and a dress shirt. Understandably he had been home in pyjamas all day, and in surprise I asked him where he was going. He had been practicing that very song, *Little Things* by One Direction for months to ask a girl to his prom. He had signed up to sing it that night at his school coffee house. In the nightmare we were living, I had completely forgotten about the coffee house he was planning to sing at that evening. Nicholas insisted he perform the song that Thursday evening, and it broke my heart to try and talk him out of it gently. Still, he insisted he wanted to perform, and so I told him I would go with him despite the fact we were still in shock. Nicholas performed beautifully and it was a powerful reminder at the same time of the love that Joe and I shared. More so, it spoke to me about the fortitude of our son, and his incredible resilience in the face of adversity. My son's gentle and sweet performance in the storm of our lives was a little bit of heaven on earth in the nightmare that had just begun for us. It spoke to me about the strength of our now smaller family unit of four, and the amazing things my children are capable of. In hindsight, I draw strength from this memory as one of the blessings from the incredibly special children that Joe and I created.

The song I chose for Joe at our Vow Renewal Ceremony was *A Thousand Years* by Christina Perri. This song is about eternal love and is as fitting in Joe's passing as it was in life. Christina Perri sings, *'I have died everyday waiting for you. Darling don't be afraid I have loved you for a thousand years, I'll love you for a thousand more.'*

I cherish that song and the words it says, *'one step closer.'* Each day I wake up to the sobering reality that I am alone, a little piece of me dies. At the same time I am one step closer to the day I will be together again with my Beloved in Heaven.

Nine months after Joe's passing, I found the vows he wrote to me two years before. When I found these vows, I was relieved to have found them quite accidentally when looking for notes on my first book. When I read these Vows, tears streamed down my cheeks, and it reminded me of what I needed to hear: *Joe loved me*. Some of the words in the vows made more sense reading it after his death; it revealed a man who struggled in life. Unfortunately, I could not see how much Joe struggled in life until after his death. I think his words are beautiful words of truth and show what a loving, caring soul he was.

Jennifer Angelee

Here are Joe's vows to me:

My Divine Vows to My Darling Wife Jennifer

Jen, over 17 years ago I stood in front of you and promised to be your Husband, your Lover, and your Friend, in good times and bad, in sickness and in health, all the days of our lives. Jen our life together has gone from the happiest days of all, to the saddest I could ever imagine. We laughed so hard and cried even harder. I am blessed each day with the sound of your voice and the stories and dreams you tell me. You have guided me through an incredible life and I'm asking you, 'Can I continue to be in your dreams and in your soul's spirit of life?' I promise to continue to believe in you and all that you do.

Jen, when I first saw your eyes I saw your beautiful soul. Your soul lit up my soul with love, faith and hope. From the first time you gave me the faith that I would find you again. Hope that when I found you again that you would not pass me by. When I found you the second time I prayed I would never lose you again. For to fall in love with an angel like you is truly the greatest gift of all.

Jen, I have experienced the most incredible life with you that I could ever imagine. I always look forward to the time we have together and dreaded the time we are apart. To hold your hand sends tingles through my body knowing that I am loved by the most beautiful friend and lover a man could ever have. The guided knowledge you bring to my life has forever enlightened me. I promise to continue to listen and grow with you. You have shown me trust, patience, honestly. And I promise to show you the same and much more.

Jen, we share the most beautiful children together, they are the gift of life. They are extraordinary people and they have over achieved our wildest expectations. I thank you for helping me guide them on their journey of life. Your guiding light has blessed them with the knowledge to always move forward with their journey of a spiritual life and I thank you for that. I promise to help you in guiding them forward through life's good and bad, and ups and downs.

Jen, the time we have is very precious to me. Sometimes it seems to stand still and other times it moves so fast. May we find the balance of time together. Without you my life would not be complete, my heart would be broken, and my soul would be lost. I promise to be truthful to you and trusting in your words.

Jen I want to ask you to forgive me for all that I have done wrong by you. The foolish mistakes I have made, the lies and the harm I have caused you. I'm sorry for not listening to you for you have always been right. So from this point on I promise to be truthful, honest, and respectful and to protect you from the injustice the world harms you with.

Jen should I fall, I ask for your patience in getting up. And should you fall, please know that I will always be there to catch you and help you up.

Jen, take this ring as a sign of my love and fidelity for you. When you look at this ring, remember me and the love I have for you. I will always be here for you no matter what path you take. You are the light that lights my journey of life, and I can't wait to see where we end up. I LOVE YOU.

Joe's words to me are incredibly beautiful and sweet. I am humbled by his belief in me and in many ways he's fulfilling his 'divine' vows in a spiritual form by being a spiritual guide to me. In hindsight, these vows portray a man who is highly spiritual but was struggling with life. There is a sadness there that I unfortunately did not recognize at the time, because for me it was easily one of the best days of my life. The vows I wrote to Joe are not as telling of the future reality that was to come.

Joe,

I want to thank you for loving me unconditionally and for giving me the life we have. Most importantly, I want to thank you for our beautiful children ~ Nicholas, Faith, Hope and Joseph (who I hope is with us today in spirit).

We have been together 23 years and I have loved you the entire time. I get the feeling our souls have known each other thousands of years and will be together for thousands more.

You know I cannot say it has always been easy for us in this life. We have had so many struggles and challenges. However, I can honestly say that I have done everything in my power to honour our commitment and love to each other.

Let's remember the beauty and forget the bad as I stand with you today. Let us renew our strength and commitment to each other, together with our children here today. May we be a positive example to them of love, faith and hope and endurance of the human spirit.

We are blessed to be here on this beautiful day, at this beautiful place, together. I don't want to forget this moment. I will tuck it into my soul for eternity.

May our belief and our faith push us forward in all the days of our lives and may our souls freely be together forever.

I love you. Together with Nicholas, Faith and Hope, we love you.

Please take this kiss from me upon your cheek as a symbol of my love, commitment and affection.

May we be blessed with peace and harmony all the days to come. Amen.

Chapter 6

In Search of My Rose

"A rose's rarest essence lives in the thorn." - Rumi

If there ever was such a thing as hell, I experienced it for months after Joe's death. So much negativity happened in those first awful months after the funeral, I recall it like I was at the bottom of a deep, dark pit, but each thing I did, brought me one step closer to awakening to my higher self and greater purpose. My soul was evolving and ascending.

Since the death of our son, Joseph, communicating with those on the other side was a familiar concept to me. I just never thought I would be communicating with my husband on the other side at such a young age, after such a tragic death.

My family upbringing was not spiritual beyond what was taught in church and besides knowing that my grandmother had seen my grandfather just a few days after his death, my mother warned me about psychics and mediums. She didn't trust or believe in them, and her being brought up in the very traditional church's viewpoint, her mind was not open to others who received information from the other side from any person not personally related. I therefore kept my readings private from my family. I knew Joe's family had a few stories of eerie events around deceased loved ones, but they were not likely to visit mediums themselves that I was aware of.

As time passed after Joe's death, I began to examine the concept of mediumship from a higher level and from a Christ-like perspective. Two years after Joe's death, my faith in Christianity heightened as I saw Christ's life with a fresh perspective and as a metaphor to my experiences.

The second Easter after Joe's death, I began to see Jesus' crucifixion and more importantly the Ascension of Christ with clarity. I marvelled at the gospel stories when Jesus appeared to his disciples and spoke of love, heaven, God the father and the Holy Spirit. It took Jesus 40 days to ascend back to the father in heaven. Ten days later, the Holy Spirit appeared at Pentecost to all of the disciples and to Mary Magdalene. Jesus spoke of the importance of love and his home in heaven. Yet the Bible also warns of communication with the dead and seers who prophesize the future. Of course there are earthbound spirits and those who cause mischief, who I am in no way suggesting that we seek to interact with. But my husband brought to me messages of love for life, similar to Jesus, that I cannot perceive having done anything unholy.

The messages my Beloved brought to me reinforced and enhanced the Christian values and beliefs that we are all one and that love is everlasting. The Bible describes five times where Jesus appeared to his disciples, at one time to 500 people who saw him at once.

Why did Jesus return to Earth after his resurrection? First, to convince his disciples that he was alive. Second, to comfort and reassure them that they had a future. Thirdly, Jesus appears to commission them to spread the good news to the world.

Jesus accomplished this in forty days and after Pentecost, the Christian Church with new beliefs of heaven and love evolved. Interestingly, in my healing from grief and in my mediumship journey, there is a pattern in my readings from my Beloved which serve the same three purposes. First, my husband appears to let me know that he is alive and that his love for the kids and I is still the same as it was on Earth. Second, to comfort me; as time passes, Joe's communication with me expands beyond proving his existence and comforting me personally. He brings forth information on the ascension of the soul, the expansion of love into God Source, piercing concepts of limiting life beliefs, and the power of everlasting love.

The day after the funeral I contacted Cheryl to take her up on her offer for the free reading. Nervously I called with her card in one hand, the phone in the other.

She answered, "Hi Cheryl?"

"Helloo! I have been waiting for you!" she replied.

We arranged for a time. I don't even remember what day of the week it was by then, but a few days later this bubbly blonde psychic from the U.S. was at my door ready to chat up a storm. Her positive energy provided relief from the desperation I was feeling. I had been kicked down so many times over that past week; I was battered and bruised on the inside from the emotional assaults I was victim to. I felt shame since I was the closest person to Joe. Surely they felt it had to be my fault.

Cheryl was the first advocate for me. She not only delivered messages from Joe, she pulled me together as much as she could in one afternoon. The first thing she burst forth with was, "Honey this man loves you. He talked my ear off the whole 45 minute drive. I had to turn my radio off! Now I've never done this before, but he keeps showing me something beside your bed, something to do with a rose or roses. Can I go upstairs and look in your bedroom? What he's telling me about is in the corner of your bedroom beside your bed."

"Sure." I said, "Be my guest." I led Cheryl to our master bedroom in a daze not thinking much about what she was talking about. Slowly, she looked around the room.

"There it is!" she said as she discovered the framed wedding picture in the corner of the wall beside *my* side of the bed. What she was referring to was no ordinary object.

One Christmas years before, Joe carved this large beautiful picture frame with roses and vine-like stems. On the bottom of the frame he carved the words: *"In Search of My Rose."* He placed an 8x10 wedding photo of us with his arms wrapped around my waist and his adoring eyes looking at me as I starred down into my bouquet of roses. He bordered the photo with red velvet matting. He even etched the glass that overlaid the picture and the red velvet. When he gave it to me, it was such an over the top romantic gesture, as a young mother; it made me a little uncomfortable. I didn't know how to receive such a gift. Unfortunately, I was young and naïve and I did not appreciate the depth of emotion and special thoughtfulness that Joe put into this gift he made.

The rose thing didn't quite make sense to me. I remember Joe explaining to me that I was his *"rose, and he had searched his whole life until he found me."* In hindsight, it makes all the more sense and often Joe will pass messages to mediums for me with a rose reference. He has even had a Reiki Master smell roses during my healing session without her being aware of my connection. Even if there is an unclear message about a rose in a group reading, I know it is my Beloved.

Cheryl was like a kid finding a treasure on a hidden treasure hunt. She drew my attention to the picture on the wall, "He says his energy is on the picture because he made it. He said whenever you want to connect with him or feel him, look at this picture."

"Funny," I said, "I've been waking up staring at it each morning".

Cheryl and I made our way into my kitchen. We sat at the kitchen table as the spring sun shined in the window and I began taping the session anxious to hear from my Beloved.

Cheryl: Your aura has been leaking all over. You have been attacked by everybody; you're giving out all your energy. *(Drawing her attention briefly to my family members)* You have always been the rock in the family. Your kids are unbelievably gifted and have lived many lives. Your children are very strong and will overcome, they love their father. Joe was not as strong as they are. He hears all the good now. The children have also talked to Joe. He says your children will be your strength forever; they will always be your best friends.

He's saying, "It's okay to lean on them."

Me: I feel guilt for what I said to Joe three days prior to his death. I had said that, "The kids are more mature than him."

Cheryl: None of it matters now. *(Cheryl and I discussed my daughter Faith).* Faith has unbelievable grounding skills and has the ability to talk to any spirits she wants.

Joe will not leave it alone. He keeps saying, "Please forgive me for leaving the way that I did." He tried to stop but had taken it too far and it was too late. Joe could have pulled out of his low mood. You need to get rid of the guilt because you did nothing wrong. You were just being you.

While we sat in the kitchen during the reading, Nicholas came home from school because he forgot his lunch. His timing was serendipitous. Nicholas had been through unbelievable trauma and Cheryl also had messages for Nicholas from his Dad.

Cheryl to Nicholas: Your Dad is very much at peace. He's showing me a boat; someday you will have a completely peaceful feeling with this boat on the water. Your Dad is also showing me a remote control boat…

I told her that Nicholas has one of those.

Cheryl: Your Dad is saying to you Nicholas, "When you put that boat on the water, and feel that peace, that's you and me buddy."

Cheryl told Nicholas that Joe was also showing her a car, a black Mustang. Nicholas had been building a model of a Mustang with his Dad. Nicholas had put it in the casket, but since the casket was closed at the wake, Cheryl could not have known this. Nicholas even finished the car by himself at the last minute and added the stickers by himself. He was surprised at what a good job he did without his Dad.

Cheryl: Your Dad says that you're going to build another one and that one day that shiny black car will be yours.
Your Dad is completely at peace. There is no more pain for him whatsoever. He's just floating around up there.

Joe continued to communicate with Nicholas.

Cheryl: Your Dad says to you, "I'm sorry you have had to be the rock."

Cheryl to Me: Joe is a very visual person, an artsy, creative soul. Does one of your kids play with a ball? Joe is showing me a ball rolling. He's showing a picture with young children playing ball.

Me: Um, one of the girls just started playing soccer last night.

Cheryl: He was there at that time. He will be present in your lives like a guardian angel. He will be with you forever if you like…

Joe keeps showing me the number ten. The number ten is very significant to you…

Me: Yes, that's me, my birthday is 10/10.

Cheryl explained how Joe couldn't talk before, but he was able to talk and communicate and give symbols.

Cheryl: He's giving the rose, the number ten. Please do not dare feel guilty about the way things were left with Joe. This man has gone through emotional waves his whole life. He went through highs, where he would bring it all in and then drop. Don't ever feel like it's anything you said or did because you guys are always in your happy place. He adores you guys so much; he's going to be your guardian angel forever.

He says third time is a charm. He said that lesson is learned and that we are growing from this, next time you will all be together and continue to be happy together.

Cheryl was saying that in my next life with Joe, there would be the harmony that this life and a past life did not provide. At the time, I still had questions around the past lives that Joe and I shared. Had we only had one past life together? To me our love seemed like we had shared an even greater history. I later came to realize that what Cheryl meant by "third time is a charm" is the synchronicity of our suicides. In a past life, I had been the one to take my life, he in this life. In our next life, we would be happy together, appreciating our eternal love and life.

Cheryl: God pushes us to where we need to be. Nicholas, you are so strong; you are a rock and a cougar, buddy. (*To me*) Your children are all spiritually gifted, and Nicholas was the person chosen to find his Dad. Joe says to Nicholas, "You are my hero!" Nicholas is going to be a great father, and when you are all together again, he might even be the Dad. Third time is a charm, and when this life is completed, it will seem like nothing but a bad dream.

Now we need to work on earthly things and be strong because you have a long road ahead. In the end it is going to seem like a small, bad dream. You guys could not cure him, and whatever happens to the rest of you, you will never be depressed like him.

(Cheryl looking at Nicholas) I know you're worried about your Mom, but whatever happens to your Mom, she will never get so down that she cannot get back up. Your Mom is going to have people in your life that are a lot more positive.

Cheryl mentioned Nicholas' grandfather, Joe's Dad. Cheryl said that Joe was showing her a ring he wears on his right hand. Cheryl continued to look at Nicholas reassuringly. "Don't worry, nobody's going to get in, don't worry about your Mama. There are things you can do to protect yourself and there's only certain people you can elevate. Know the difference and focus on those who are positive."

Cheryl to Me: Shield yourself everyday and wrap yourself in white light to protect yourself from lower energies. You are the only one who knows who you truly are, that is open and affectionate. In past lives, we were healers; you are a healer! Your future is counselling people, this is your purpose here on Earth.

Me: Joe was supporting me with my purpose in whatever way he could.

Cheryl: Joe pushed me to you to make sure that you stay on your destiny and keep going. This experience of loss is going to open up doors for you. It is going to open up three doors, one to spiritual support, two to being an entrepreneur. Third, is a book that you are writing. It will be finished and there will be two.

The book I was writing is *Miracles of Love, Faith and Hope,* published the following year. The second book she was referring to was this one, *Beloved, I Can Show You Heaven.*

Cheryl: In two years, you will have all your ducks in a row. Your energy is scattered. Honey, you take on the world. Use your psychic gifts to help yourself and others.

Cheryl drew me a picture of my guardian angel and I thought it looked like me.

I began to get upset as Cheryl was describing how negative people were affecting my relationship with Joe. She assured me that my emotions were only me picking up on other people's negativity and Joe's suicidal feelings, that there is nothing wrong with me. Cheryl reiterated, "This man brought me across town, he literally pulled me, my husband did not bring me to the funeral home; your husband did! He says he's been madly in love with you since he was nineteen. You and he have such love, you can go through so much bullshit together and nothing and nobody is going to slow you down and stop you now because now that Joe is where he is, he has your back better than he ever has. You wait and see, he's still your family, forever. God brought you these children. They are all you need and he's watching out for you guys."

Cheryl: He showed me his demise. This was supposed to happen. It actually went further than it did with the other life. Don't let anyone hurt you or affect your spirit anymore. You need to be the warrior.

Me: Even though he says it was an accident, was he meant to die this way in this life?

Cheryl: In this life, yes.

Me: (*weakly*) He did so much, but he always felt helpless.

Cheryl: I asked spirit, "I am interested to see how I am connected to you and your kids".... I am hearing the words: "because we are in a book together."

Me: We are in a book together? Hmmm.

Cheryl: (*slowly*) We have been in a book together, a story that's been told in a book. I'm interested to see how that unfolds.

    Cheryl explained how I carried Joe's depression and darkness, and that I would be happier in the next few years. By sacrificing himself, he was freeing us in this lifetime. Joe knew he had to pass before me.

Cheryl: Jen, you will never be dark again. In this particular life, his demon was beyond him, and because you are spiritual, he passed it to you. You took on the demon of him, and he saw it happening. He had to think in his mind, I know it would be devastating for my family to lose me, but my wife and my family will be completely demolished if I stay. He sacrificed himself for the greater good, how he did it had no meaning to his demise and now you're going to be happier, you're going to be healthier and you're coming into the Jenny you used to be.

I expressed one of the first feelings I had days after Joe died, despite the sadness. One of the first feelings I felt is that he gave me back to myself.

Cheryl: You and your son will never have to see the demons; Joe said you would have all drowned in that boat. Right now I know it stings, but he saved you all. He saved your life…He brought me through so much to bring this message to you guys, but I want you to know, that's what happened… He showed me everything but it was his time and this was his gift to give to you guys, and sweetheart you are a light, you're such a positive person, and that darkness was never yours to wear. You will never feel that way again. You were carrying that demon, and now you're hurting the normal hurt. When I met you that day, I already felt relief when I gave you that message, for whatever reason, he found *me* to give these messages to you.

Me: Uh-hmm…I'm grieving.

Cheryl: You're going to say to me in the future, Cheryl, I'm the happiest I've ever been in my entire life, how can this be?
Things will start to lift, I cannot say it will be tomorrow, or even a month from now, but things will start to shift.

I continued to express my guilt about the conversations I had with Joe. Cheryl said, "There is no guilt."
As Nicholas left to go back to school after his lunch, I told Cheryl, "His Dad has brought Nicholas so many friends to support him."
As Cheryl ate a chocolate covered strawberry from the edible arrangement that was sent to me during her visit I told her how chocolate strawberries are my favourite and it's the sweetest thing I've had since he passed.

Cheryl: Joe has brought so many things here today: he brought us your son, these strawberries..., and he is showing me the number ten again, how else do you connect with the number ten sweetheart?

As I made another cup of coffee for Cheryl I said, "I am Jen ten! If I had a personalized license plate it would be that, I am the tenth person born in my family, when I was a child I lived at the address which is my birthday...."

Cheryl: Did I give you the confirmation now?

Me: Oh yes, (*jokingly*), He used to call me the perfect ten. He knows how I feel about the number ten.

Cheryl: You are the perfect ten, sweetheart. That is true and I'm so glad I can give you peace in your mind, to help you go on.

I went on to explain what had happened with his family on the Mother's day three days before his death and how Joe reacted. Cheryl continued to reassure me. She said that Joe was dealing with this his whole life.

Cheryl: When I say a demon, I'm not kidding with you. When you said you felt his suicidal thoughts and feelings, these were coming from the dimension you understand. I see things from a higher dimension, and I can tell you, you were feeling his demons. That was not you.

Me: And he is okay now?

Cheryl: Oh, he is in a beautiful place.

Cheryl read my bracelet, "Hope, Faith, Love..."
I explained to her how that is my book, *Miracles of Love, Faith and Hope* and how my kids each taught me about these virtues. "Nicholas is my love."
"Ooh!" She said.
As Cheryl was getting prepared to leave, she did an angel card reading. She told me I will find love again. Just as she said that, the Marriage Card

fell on the floor. Tears came to my eyes, "Will I ever marry again? Don't we only have one soul mate? Can I ever love anyone else?"

Cheryl assured me I would find love again and I wouldn't have to go looking for it.

Cheryl said that blue light is around me and my guardian angels said to put blue opal light around me. Lastly, I got the card, "*There is nothing to worry about. You are safe in this situation, all you have to do is ask, and the outcome flows through you.*"

Chapter 7

The Sharpest Thorns

"They that love beyond the world cannot be separated by it. Death cannot kill what never dies." ~ *William Penn*

Evening of May 26, 2015 – Reading with Greg

Despite Cheryl's words of comfort, and the peace she brought to our home, the sting of our loss grew more painful each day. The reality hit and each time I woke I felt like hell's hands were pushing me down square in the chest.

It was only four days after Cheryl's reading on May 26, 2015, that I brought Hope to the first soccer game of the season. I struggled to ground myself that beautiful cool, sunny spring evening. The game was on the east side of town and I became lost in the unfamiliar neighbourhood trying to find the park. At last we arrived, and I quickly found Hope's coach and introduced her. Before I knew it, Hope was on the field and the absence of Joe hit me like a rock. I felt the pain of having a daughter in soccer without a father. It hit me hard and broke my heart, because unlike all previous years of my kid's soccer, hockey, and ball games, Joe was present as the adoring father who sometimes coached the kids; this would be no more. I felt so sorry for my daughter and what she would be missing out on. This was coupled with the fact that from this secluded park resting on the north side of town, we could see Joe's work, prominently in the distance. Everything reminded me of Joe. Even Hope's soccer team was sponsored by his company and this was printed boldly on her shirt and on her soccer water bottle.

My heart ached and I felt restless. I paced as I called Greg for the first time. I brought his number with me, just in case I had a chance to call and book a reading with him. He had done an informal reading for me in my first book, and I met him once or twice in the summer about five years previous at a Mediumship Meet up. I had acquired his number the previous summer when I was writing the Miracles book in order to ask him permission to share my reading with him in my book. Fortunately, Greg answered my call and we arranged for him to do a reading for me that evening when the kids were settled in bed. I did not tell him who I wanted to connect with but was so relieved to have secured a reading with him.

That May evening I sat down at the kitchen table with my phone on record, my note paper and a pen. I was anxious to hear from my husband.

During this first reading with Greg, Joe brought through his emotion of remorse with Greg.

Greg: I am getting a male on the other side. He is feeling horrible about the fact that he has left you and you alone with the kids. He said that he was brought up believing it was a sign of weakness for a guy to share his feelings in a sensitive way.

Are there two younger kids and a big age difference with an older kid?

Me: Yes, there is a 17 year old and two younger girls, age 12 and 8.

Greg: He's saying, "It is important to look on the two younger ones a lot," though I get the feeling you already know this. He is watching over them as well, but of course it's not the same thing from where he is at. He said he is concerned for the two younger ones. He sees them playing a lot but he is concerned for them. He said just because they are not showing signs of anything, does not mean they are not experiencing it.

Is your older son quite sensitive or intuitive?

Me: Yes, why? What do you mean?

Greg: The older one will be able to pick up when his Dad is around. He is actually going to be more okay with this. It is going to be hard for him, but being able to pick up on things is going to make it a bit easier for him.

Me: Hmm. My older girl was channelling him recently, my 12 year old. They are all spiritually gifted in their own way.

Greg: The 12 year old might be a little bit scared about it?

Me: Yeah.

Greg: Where as the 17 year old is more okay with it.

Me: He did not used to be. He is more open-minded now.

Greg: Check in on the younger two more than him. There might be nights where your daughters or son want to sleep with you in the same bed.

Me: Yes, my younger daughter said last night, "I cannot go to sleep without you lying with me." Actually, I just said she never wanted to sleep with her older sister until a couple of nights ago.

Greg: Okay. Let's see what else I'm getting...He said you're okay, that you're a very strong person. Not to diminish what it is you're going through here.

Me: Yes, it aches, it hurts, for sure.

Greg: Oh for sure, ah...He's telling me it is hard all day for you, but you particularly feel it at night and in the morning than during the day. He's saying that your room feels particularly lonely and empty at night. He says you have feelings of being isolated and alone at night. He says he is going through the exact same thing even though he has crossed over. Earlier I was picking up on both of your emotions. They are almost perfectly matched.

    At night he lies with you on the bed, and he is getting kind of intimate here but I'm going to give it to you as I get it, okay?

Me: Okay (*apprehensively*).

Greg: He spoons with you.

Me: I don't feel anything, though I am pretty sensitive. I don't feel it.

Greg: He's telling me that and he wants you to know this is happening and it's hard to feel his presence but he wants you to know that this is happening.
   When you're lying there at night, do you ever feel like a breeze go by your cheek?

Me: Maybe.

Greg: Okay, be on the lookout for that. Be open to that. It will be like a slight coincidence or whatever but there will be no explanation for it, when you feel that, that's him.

Me: I have felt the covers move around my heart centre. It's so fast. It feels like someone slightly adjusted the blanket over me.

Greg: Yes, yes, that's definitely him.

Me: Can we go back to something I'm hung up on?

Greg: Yup.

Me: The days before were rough, for both of us and I feel like from the things I said that I inadvertently led him into this.

Greg: Okay, I'm getting that his passing was medically related.

Me: Ah, kind of… not in an obvious way.

Greg: No, I'm not getting blood pressure or heart because I'm asking those questions and he's saying *no*. Ahh, okay…. He's saying like an accident?

Me: Kind of, maybe. *(In distress and apprehension)* He hung himself. I kind of feel like he went through the motions and he did not mean for it to happen.

Greg: Okay, I'm going to check in on him on this…..Yeah, No, You're absolutely right. He didn't mean for that to happen at all!

Me: Ah shit! (*In an agonizing groan*).

Greg: He's telling me he was alone in the house when it happened.

Me: Well, I was sleeping.

Greg: Okay, well in that sense he was saying he was alone because you could not have known, that you could not have stopped him. That's why he is saying he was alone because he's removing you from any responsibility for what happened.

Me: But, did anything I said or do lead to that? In the previous days…?

Greg: I'm just going to tell you what he's telling me, that he has had a long history of depression and anxiety.

Me: Okay. (I take a deep breath and sigh).

    Greg listens and sighs hard, listening to Joe, repeating "Okay".

Greg: It's nothing to do with anything you would have said or done. He's saying….

Me: Because I was not lovey-dovey the days before, but I was frustrated with him.

Greg: Well, yeah. All couples go through that. It doesn't matter; all couples go through highs and lows.

Me: He never asked for help.

Greg: He was never open about talking about stuff. You would bring it up and he's laughing about it now saying you would bring it up and he would say, "Yeah we'll talk about it but just not right now", or he would pretend to listen but he's not really listening; and he would never offer any suggestions or anything to move things forward, so he's admitting to all this stuff.

Me: Um-hmm.

Greg: Ahhh, He really does feel badly about all that. He wants you to know, and it will still be hard after our conversation, but he doesn't want you to take any blame or feel responsible for what's happened. And he's very emotional while he's telling me there is no way you can take responsibility for his actions. I mean that if someone is that determined, they are going to do it.

Me: I mean I didn't think that was going to happen, so I did not try to stop it.

Greg: Well, I don't know if you could have anyway. He is a pretty stubborn guy and he's agreeing. He's saying, "Yeah, I'm totally stubborn."

Within Greg's reading, I was seeking the answers I desperately needed to make sense of Joe's suicide. I was looking for a reason, anything to put the pieces of this horrendous puzzle together. I too felt like pieces of myself, scattered in all directions. The space in between each piece was my Beloved and I missing each other. The reading went deeper as Joe tried to communicate through Greg about all the things I had been wondering about in the previous days.

Greg: Let's see what else I'm getting. He's going back to the fight or the argument that you guys had. He wants to just clear the air on stuff. You said you want to sell the house, or something?

Me: I only vaguely remember that I may have said something in the heat of a moment. I hope he did not take it the wrong way.

Greg: He wants you to know that he knows that you really didn't mean that and he wants to clear the air that it did not lead up to what he did. When all that was happening, did you ask him to sleep in a separate room or somewhere else?

Me: He always slept somewhere else because he was working nights. The night before he died, I was so fed up I rejected his apology because I was at my wits end. I feel very guilty. I have never been like that before. I feel like I broke his heart. I was just doing it to protect myself.

Greg: He says he deserved that because even with his apologies it still was not moving the situation further ahead because there was no resolution.

Me: It was too little, too late. It always was. He would always apologize after he majorly screwed up.

Greg: Yeah, but things would not change. Okay, thank you Joe. There is something very important and special that he wants you to have. It's almost like the shape of a card. It's really, really special.

Me: Yes, but I don't know where it is. This is what I think it is: When we started going out he showed me a picture he drew in grade 8 of the girl of his dreams, and when he showed me the picture, I could not believe how much it looked like me. It was a sketch and it was on a square piece of paper.

Greg: Yes, yes, yes! That is what it is.

Me: I wondered the other night where it is. He has so much stuff; I cannot even touch his stuff.

Greg: There is no rush but he wants you to know that the feelings he had then are what he has now. Everything for him is still the same in that respect. In fact he's saying he loves you even more now than he did then, so when you do come across it, and you will…

Me: But can he tell me where it is? I feel it's like his shop in the basement. It's not easy to find, he's got so much stuff.

Beloved, I Can Show You Heaven

Greg: Right - he was a collector.

Me: He was a collector and he was secretive about his stuff. (Starting to cry). My heart breaks. Was it supposed to be like this? This is not the way I imagined our lives, you know I thought we were going to grow old together.

Greg: He's saying that he did not imagine things to be this way either, and he's feeling very awful about it…. And he wishes he could turn the clock back.

Me: Yeah, so do I.

Greg: He loves you just as much now; actually he loves you more than before. He says he really misses you.

Me: I feel the same way.

Greg: And he says he really loves you a lot. Do you ever see things like your two hearts beat together as one?

Me: Yeah, I feel that. I feel that. I feel like I want my heart to be cut out of my body. I don't know how to describe it, my heart hurts so much. It hurts so much I just want it out. It hurts to have a heart.

Greg: Well, of course. He wants you to know that he is with you all the time, even if you don't feel his presence there all the time. He was also with you at the game with the kids, he was with you in the car….he's saying he's always with you.

Me: I missed having him in the car in the seat beside me. (Deep sigh) I'm scared about my life.

Greg: In what way?

Me: I hate feeling so… I hate not having him around. I miss him so much. I hate the way I'm feeling. I hate the way I feel all the time. I feel so overwhelmed by all the physical things. He did so much. He cleaned the floors. I hate not having anyone to share my life with and just having the kids and nobody else.

Greg: Oh, no, you totally will. It will take some time, but you will, and he's alright with that too. He's saying that he doesn't want to hold you back from your happiness.

Me: He loves me that much.

Greg: Okay he's giving me something here. Is there a sweater or shirt of his that has his smell on it?

Me: Yup.

Greg: He wants you to have that by your side.

Me: It's an old work shirt. I smelled it and said, 'nobody wash this' and threw it on the master bedroom closet floor. It's hard to look at but…

Greg: He wants you to sleep with it. He's getting emotional. He says it's the closest thing to let you know that he's there. He says it will help.

Me: Not the same though, but you're so specific, I know its Joe saying it. But we were together since I was 18 and it's really hard for me even to imagine he's there physically. It hurts too much (holding back tears).

Maybe this helps though because maybe I will believe he's there. It's so hard because of the way he died, there was no emotional intimacy, wasn't like he was on his death bed, dying of cancer. There was no closure. He just continued in spirit. I don't know what he was thinking (deep breath) but I feel blamed.

Greg: The unfortunate thing is that it is really easy for some to work through their grief when they have someone to blame.

Me: Well it's not like anyone came flocking to me saying they were sorry and that I was the victim. It was like I was the perpetrator. I felt accused instead of being comforted.

Greg: Well, that is very unfortunate, and it's not uncommon that it happened but you are in no way responsible for his death. For some, it is harder to hold him accountable for his death because it would make it tougher on them emotionally, if that makes sense? He's getting very emotional as I'm saying this and he's listening. If they have someone else to channel their emotions to, it makes it easier for them.

When one goes through the grieving process, there isn't just one emotion but all the emotions. There are periods of joy, sadness, anger, frustration. As I'm saying this he's saying "If you want to yell at him, go ahead. He's okay with it." He's crying and he does not hold you personally responsible for yelling at him, calling him names and stuff. He understands that this is part of the grieving process and he's responsible for you feeling what you're feeling and the emotions you're going through.

He feels responsible for this, okay, and it's important for you to know that. In no way are you responsible for this. He's taking full responsibility for what he's done and what he's putting you and your kids through, and he feels horrible; and he feels the void that's there between you and him and him and the kids.

Me: Uh-hmm.

Greg: He wants you to know that things will not go away fully, but things will get easier. But it takes time.

Me: How so? But will it be okay?

Greg: The emotional part will get easier. There will be moments when things will feel okay, embrace those moments. It's hard but it's important to try. Just embrace it. Just allow the feelings you're experiencing.

You know you're going to get some people who are going to say, 'You know you should be over this by now', or, 'It's not that bad'. The reason they say these things is because they don't understand it. They are not sure what they can say that will be comforting because most people are not taught how to handle grief, and most people try to run from it because they do not know what to say. There is no set period of time that things should be dealt with. There is no rush for things like going through his personal stuff. You may not want to look at that stuff for years.

Me: My friend said it took her a year to clean out her husband's closet.

Greg: I know some women that have taken longer that that. And there is no right or wrong or set time. He wants to support you as much as he can from where he is.

Me: How can he do that?

Greg: There will be moments you will feel his presence. Let me go back here with him again and see what else I get....Okay, right. There is something very strong here. I don't know if you've experienced this or not, but if you haven't, be aware that when you're sleeping, that's when we're the most psychic. He comes to you when you're sleeping and when you're sleeping he talks to you and whispers. He's been whispering to you and what you hear is 'shhhwhhhshhh' but he is actually telling you stuff.

Me: Okay, yeah, you know when your ear gets that inner pitch?

Greg: Yes.

Me: Sometimes my ear gets that, but maybe I don't notice when I'm sleeping.

Greg: Yes, that's him.

Me: I think I heard something the other night. I heard like a scream lying in Hope's bed in front of her dresser at the foot of the bed. I asked to hear him but it was upsetting and creepy.

Greg: He's apologizing for the creepy part. He was trying to get through.

Me: I'm not really scared of him. I always said he could be around me when he dies and he's the only one where I'm okay with that, but I meant it when I'm old lady, I didn't mean that he would be watching me from the other side now.

Greg: And he's protecting you and the kids also. Did anyone wipe out in the game today?

Me: Could be. I was not paying good attention, could be at school too.

Greg: Okay well, I see a grass stain or something. He wants you to know that he's watching over everybody.

Me: I don't know how I'm going to get through summer. It was going to be such a good summer with him.

Greg: He wants you to go out.

Me: It's going to be so hard for me. We were in the process of putting together the pool house. He had days to finish it.

Greg: (Concentrating) When you're lying in bed, do you ever feel that there is someone there playing with your hair? Be aware of that. You might feel tingling. He said he strokes your hair. He's hugging you around your chest area. He's saying to be aware of that. Okay, let's see: He says you have called out to him in anger?

Me: I don't think out loud but in my head.

Greg: He wants you to know that he heard that even though it was telepathically in your head. He hears your thoughts inside your mind. And when you ask if he's there, he's there. He crying and getting very emotional. He says it's very hard for him to hear these things because he's trying very hard to get your attention. He wants you to know that he hears all this.

Me: When I'm driving in the car and I hear a song, it makes me feels like it's him talking to me or I'm talking to him, you know?

Greg: Uh-huh.

Me: So he's probably there when I'm driving in the car?

Greg: Yes for sure.

Me: So we've probably spent more time together than normal.

Greg: Yes, under these unfortunate circumstances, yes.
 Let me see what else I can get here. He's saying something about a locket or necklace or something?

Me: Well today I realized that he wore a gold cross and accidentally buried it with him. I also wore a heart necklace, it was the first gift he gave me.

Greg: Yes, that is what he is referring to. He's also very touched that you kept that gold cross with him.

Me: Yeah, it was an accident but okay.

Greg: Well, he's laughing but he's happy for the accident. He said it's so insignificant in the scheme of things.
 Let me see what else (pauses). He said he had a secret pet name for you but he won't tell me what it is. Was he secretive about this kind of stuff? (the names?)

Me: Oh probably. He was very secretive.

Greg: He wants you to know that you were the love of his life, and he should have told you along time ago and he should have told you many, many times and you are so incredibly special to him, and he says you know it but he wishes he said this to you. He says he could never wish for anybody better than you.

Me: Uh-huh. I know that he felt that way.

Greg: But he's crying when he says this and laughing at the same time. He wonders why you ever put up with his quirkiness, his quirky things.

Me: (laughing) Why not? Ahhhh, I'd do anything. Does he know where my life is going to go? This really sucks, because I was not planning for this. I was content, maybe not happy. I did not want for much more. I had dreams and desires, but I did not want them at this cost.

Greg: I know things are hard, but things are going to get easier.

Me: It changes the entire dynamic of my life. He made my life easier so I could focus on what I wanted. He was so devoted, and I often did not feel well, and he would just, ah, you know pick up the slack all the time.

Greg: Things are going to be different for sure. What's important is you don't push yourself. Don't put benchmarks or timelines on anything. Every day is a different day. Every moment is a different moment. So live moment to moment. So if the moment dictates that you're feeling sad, feel sad, if your feeling angry, feel angry. If you have energy, then do something that you have energy to do. It's not something you'll notice in a week or two weeks but, for example, when you look back six months from now, that's when you'll see the changes that have happened.

Me: What about my life purpose? Will that change as well?

Greg: That will evolve in time.

Me: But will he help it?

Greg: Absolutely.

Me: Will he pull strings unlike before?

Greg: He will be working, putting things into motion from the other side. He has that commitment to you.

Me: We always travelled together, now with the kids, I don't think I can do it by myself.

Greg: He will be with you.

Me: We always did vacations together, and ….

Greg: He wants you to go and only when you're ready, and he'll be there. He says you don't really drive on the highway, eh? You stick closer to home. You won't really venture out if he's not part of the equation.

Me: Yes, I would not venture out to Montreal by myself and we were going to go this summer. I would never trust myself. I would help him, but I would probably screw us up, you know. He was just better at stuff.

Greg: Do you have a support circle? If you join a support group that might not be a bad thing.

Me: Yes, I went to someone today for suicide loss.

Greg: He's with you all the time. You're not responsible and he does not hold you responsible. If someone is healthy, the stuff that you guys argued about or whatever, would not have someone go and do something like that.

Me: I wondered if I tipped him over, or something.

Greg: No, I think it was building and what he has done was an accident.

Me: (groan) That's so sad.

Greg: Yeah, he did not mean to go and do that.

Me: It's sad.

Greg: Do you have any more questions for him?

Me: Cheryl said at the funeral home that 'Your second book is going to be better than your first'. What about all of the things I wanted to do such as my book? It's going to be more difficult because I'm a single Mom now.

Greg: Are you journaling? Because he tells me you've stopped journaling.

Me: I did write something on Sunday night.

Greg: He says put the book thing aside and start journaling right now. Put your thoughts on paper. It's going to help with the healing process, and then you'll look back and, he's correcting me… You're going to use this towards the next book and what you're going to put together next. He mentioned about the spiritual group that you want to put together. This experience now is going to help that.

Me: Yes, go on.

Greg: This experience now will definitely help with that and you will be helping other people that will be going through something similar or something different but you'll still be able to bring this into that.

It's not going to be one thing. He says you're scattered. Your ideas are all over the place. You have many different ideas and you have different pots on the stove that you're currently working on. So you're thinking that you're going to put all your energy into one thing. He said scrap that. He said that doesn't even make sense, but that being said you are definitely going to do something business-wise on its own but don't put any timelines and deadlines on it because everything is going to unfold as it needs to. Okay, and everything has its purpose and everything has it's time; and because everything has it's time, you cannot rush that time, if that makes sense.

Me: (softly listening) Um-hum, yeah. (Deep breath) I wish I had time with him in the summer. I'm going to miss seeing him in the pool; he was such a beautiful swimmer.

Greg: Like a dolphin?

Me: Yeah…What about looking for a book publisher?

Greg: Those things will take time. Remember Dr. Seuss' words: He finally found a publisher crazy enough to publish his books. These things take time so do it when you feel ready to do it. The first one may not be the one; it doesn't mean that your stuff isn't worth publishing.

Me: Well there are hundreds that I have to apply for. He was going to help me with the technical part and now, I don't know how it will get done.

Greg: And you might end up writing a book about this experience too, and that will help a whole ton of people, for sure...

Me: I'm not sure what angle to put on it, you know?

Greg: The whole thing will unfold as it needs to in time. It is not something that needs to be rushed.

Me: This could be a book – the dialogue (laughing).

Greg: For sure!

Me: I once read a book about a woman whose son died by suicide and she began seeing a medium and it was interesting.

Greg: And you know there is no time on the other side.

Me: And time goes so slow now, it used to go so fast. Especially at night the time goes so slow.

Greg: Yeah, just be okay with the time going so slow.

Me: If I had a book like that, you could be our Medium. We could record these readings and I could transcribe them. It's different with a husband than a son. With a son, it's more of a spiritual connection. With a husband it is such a physical connection, uh, but I think it would be very romantic.

I remember when we were young we cuddled and watched the movie *Ghost* and I remember we were both balling. I told my son the other night, there is an old movie called *"Ghost"* with Patrick Swayze, Demi Moore, and Whoopi Goldberg.

So I think this would be an incredibly romantic book. You know there are so many books now about heaven and the afterlife and I've never seen a love story.

Greg: (Thoughtfully) Yeah. That's true.

Me: On April 29th, two weeks before, I went to a really good Medium and I connected with Joseph, and my son said "Oh Mommy, Heaven is just like you said." And I was thinking about an idea for the name, *"Mommy I Can Show you Heaven"* for somebody who has lost a child. But for a love, I thought of *"Honey, I Can Show You Heaven"* or something.

Greg: It's really cool. He was just saying that heaven is a whole lot more than what you had said.

Me: Than what my son had said?

Greg: He says it's a whole lot more and it's a whole lot better.

Me: Has he seen our son? Has he seen Joseph?

Greg: I'm being shown a six year old. I do not know why I'm seeing a small child. Was he six when he passed or would he be six now?

Me: No, he would be sixteen.

Greg: Was your husband a jokester? Let me just see here. Oh, yeah they're hanging out. Ooh, okay. Your son is saying he brings out the kid in him!!! I was trying to figure out why he's showing me this little kid. Did your son have dark hair?

Me: Well yes he was born with dark hair. My daughters have dark hair but my son is very fair with alopecia.

Greg: Well they are together right now and he is saying that your son is definitely bringing out the kid in him.
　He's emotional and he is saying that he was very withdrawn and into himself, like a turtle in his shell. And he realizes he was always making mountains out of molehills when he was here, and he now realizes how insignificant those things were that he was making a big deal of.
　He was not willing to see it, and he says he was very stubborn and he's

getting upset and angry with himself. It's taken where he is now to open himself up, but he wishes he was able to be here and be open. He realizes how much he's missed. Ahhh, and um, he's saying how wonderful you are. He says you're very wonderful.

Me: My daughter says, "Dad is going to miss everything in our lives". I asked her if she has any questions for Dad and she said, "How could he do this?" She is a very wise, outspoken child.

Greg: He said he is not going to miss anything that they're doing. He says that they are going to miss *seeing* him there.

Me: I feel so sad for them.

Greg: He said he doesn't really have an answer for them. This comes back to that void between him and them that he described before.

Me: Hope said he used to play with him all the time when I was too busy.

Greg: Did he used to bounce her on his knee?

Me: Yeah, she was getting big for that. But he was probably the best Dad in the world. He was a fun Dad. He was very a hands-on Dad, so it's a huge loss. He was more hands-on than I ever was. Like he changed diapers and would step in and could handle more than me. He would clean up, wipe their faces and get them ready for school…He would help me with the little one when she was not listening.

Greg: She's like a little terror?

Me: She's like her Dad, very creative but articulate, and into stuff.

Greg: He just said she's like a little mini-me.

Me: Yeah, in some ways she's like a little mini-me too. Her personality is not him but what she enjoys is like him.

Greg: Is there anything else?

Me: I feel like I'm keeping you up late. I would like to keep the appointment tomorrow night if that's okay?

Greg: That's more than okay.

Me: So I would like to say goodnight to Joe (laughing a little) or would you like to say goodnight to Joe and I guess he'll be with me (laughing).

Greg: Good night Joe! Yeah, he'll definitely be with you. You okay?

Me: There are so many things, but I have to respect your time, but I really think this would be a good book. There are so many names, but I've got to think of a better name.

I also remember the name he used to call me years ago. I think its "Boo".

Greg: That's it.

Me: Good night.

Greg: Good night.

Connecting with Joe was a small break from the daunting life that lay ahead of me. It was a relief to know my husband was still there and still part of our lives, albeit in a totally different way. Joe proved himself to be involved in mine and our children's life. He was clearly okay on the other side but missing us and his old life. I missed Joe and our old life more than words can say, and I still do. So many times I wished I could just snap my fingers and bring him back. That way I would be whole again with the other half of my heart next to me in the physical.

Jennifer Angelee

Reading with Greg and Nicholas and Faith – May 27, 2015

The following evening, Greg read for me on the phone. This reading included Nicholas and Faith. Joe had many messages for the kids.

Greg: I'm connecting with Joe here. What I'm picking up is in my stomach area. There is a lot of regret, there is a lot of emotion from him. You know he never thought. He's crying here, he's really upset emotionally. He never thought about the kids having to go for therapy and the burden that you have. (Wait a sec; let me hear what he's saying).

Me: (Whispering to kids) Are you okay? If you're not, its okay to go.

Greg: He's saying he feels horrible. Um, okay, something to do with the kids, he is feeling horrible that he cannot be there as a father, he longs to hold them. He says he really longs to hold them; he wants to tell them that everything will be alright, that they will be alright.

Me: My kids are here Greg and they are getting emotional. Is this bad for them to be here? Not my baby, but my older two.

Greg: He wants them to hear this. But it is up to you and it is up to them whether they want to hear this.

Me: I think they do…

Greg: He wants them to hear this. He wants them to know that he loves them very, very much. This has nothing to do with them. What happened has everything to do with their father, with Joe, and has nothing to do with them.

Me: Okay…(*crying breath and sniffles*)

Greg: He knows they have questions. He wants them to know that they have to look after each other and it's important that they look out for each other and that they help you out around the house as well. They could be taking turns. He's saying for them to help look after you – that's really important….but keeping in balance with still being kids because that's really important.

He's saying he was teaching them how to look after themselves. He was teaching them how to help around the house and he was teaching them how to be supportive of each other.

Me: He was doing this before he passed?

Greg: Yeah, this is what he says. He was teaching them about their toys and their belongings, that they are theirs but it's important to share. He's extending that to look after their chores, and not only to each other, but to extend that to you too. He's getting emotional when he's saying this: so that you're not having to put as much of your energy into that.

He's really happy and excited that you could feel him last night.

Me: Okay (crying). Yeah I just went to bed late and said to him, "Okay, here we go Joe. Good night." But I woke up and went over to his side of the bed, and I uh ah, don't like waking up in the morning now because I don't like my days now.

Me: (Whispering to Faith and Nick) Are you okay?

Greg: He's feeling really badly about something to do with the mortgage? Is there a lot of bills and stuff?

Me: Yes there's a lot of bills and stuff coming due and there's a lot of paperwork that I have to get done. I am overwhelmed. There's transferring the automobile out of his name, and…

Greg: Okay he meant something to do with payments. He's saying there is not much to worry about with that.

Me: I know he feels bad, but can he do anything to help?

Greg: He's saying do a few each day. He's saying what is more important is the connection with 'me and his kids'. That's more important than the bills.

(*Listening*) Okay thanks, Joe. He's laughing and not to take away from the serious of all the bills but he's saying just look at a couple of bills at a time and not all at once.

Me: There's CPP and Death Benefit and all the stuff at work.

Greg: Okay, so what he's saying is to put them into different piles. So bills that need to be paid right away are one pile, insurance is another.

Me: (Sarcastically laughing). Oh wow. He's so practical. Jeez, that really helps.

Greg: He's saying just put things into different piles. He's laughing as he's saying this. This really isn't a big deal. But of course it is. He's also saying to put them into different file folders and label accordingly.

Me: Okay (Nicholas and Faith giggling at the advice).

Greg: He's saying with the kids, the younger ones; lay their clothes out the night before.

(Faith laughing because I always did that)

Me: I always do but the kids are getting so big their clothes are not fitting anymore.

Greg: He's says that you can get his parents to take them shopping. He's saying they can get ice cream and have fun. (He's feeling better now).

Me: (Laughing) Should Nicholas have a beer tomorrow night at his prom party?

Nick: Such a specific question…

Greg: Joe's laughing. He's saying, "Don't get to the point where you're staggering around."

Me: Can Joe keep an eye on him? That's an understatement because I said, 'Don't even get to the second drink.'

Faith: (Laughing). I think by the first drink he'll be staggering around.

Nick: No.

Me: Be careful.

Nick: I'll be careful.

Greg: Joe is emotionally saying to his oldest son; "You're now the man of the house, and I am very, very proud of you". And as he's saying that he has both of his hands on each of your shoulders and he is saying, "I'm so, so, so, so proud of you, and you've earned this and it's important for you to be there for your two younger ones. At the same time, go have fun and enjoy because you're now the man of the house". He says he knows that school is tough but keep going, just get through it. Don't quit, you're doing okay. No matter what, he'll always be proud of you. He's saying this is because you've been asking if he's proud of you, and he wants you to know that he's incredibly proud of you, and that has never changed. It will always be the same how very proud he is of you.

He wants you to know that he loves you so, so, so much. He hasn't really said this but he wants you to know. He really wishes he was here right now and physically saying this to you. He's hugging you really tight and he's giving you this huge bear hug and pulling you into him when he's saying this, like he's taking all the air out of you when he is hugging you so hard and so tight. He says that he gives you these big bear hugs and he's giving you one right now. He's saying this one is tighter than ever.

At this point in the reading, Nicholas, Faith and I were crying as we heard Greg say Joe's words spoken aloud.

Greg: For his daughter; this is easier said than done: He doesn't want her to be afraid. He says he hasn't changed. He's still the same person now in heaven, as he was for her. If she ever thinks she feels him around it's because he loves her. He's crying, he loves her and he loves her so incredibly much and he still wants to be able to hold her close to him. He's saying if you want to sleep with the light on, that's fine.

Jennifer Angelee

(Faith sobbing)

Me to Faith: Are you okay?

Greg: He says you're a very strong little girl and you sleeping with the light on doesn't make you a weak person.

(Faith sobbing)

Greg: He wishes he could hug all of you at the same time. He wants you all to know that this isn't any easier for him. He's not trying to take away from how difficult it is for all of you. He wants you to know that it is just as hard, or harder on him. He is going through all the same emotions and he wishes all of you were comfortable knowing he is there with you. Also he has this added burden that he's carrying that all this has happened and it's his fault with everything that has happened. He wants everybody to know that. He's laughing and he's saying he's not out to scare anyone.

Me: I know that.

Greg: But he wants all the kids to know that too.

Me: Uh-hmm. Hope needs to know that.

Greg: For some reason he's showing me a pair of pajamas or pajama bottoms. They have race cars or some kind of a pattern on them. There are cartoons or they are like kids pajama bottoms. What is he saying about that?

Oh, okay. What he is saying is he wants each of you to do something fun each evening. It could be wearing something funny, something with some uplift or some kind of humour to it. He doesn't want anyone to feel guilty for having funny moments or moments with laughter in it. He's saying that he knows you're feeling guilty if you're having funny moments that he's not there to share. He's crying. He's saying, the more funny moments you guys have, the easier it is on him. He wants you to have funny moments, the more the better.

Beloved, I Can Show You Heaven

Me: The kids are having funny moments. I'm not…

Greg: He wants you to have funny moments and share in them to. He doesn't want guilt around the funny moments.

Nick: Maybe not guilt but missing him and wishing he was there…

Greg: He wants you to know that he is there! It's not the same of course but he's there and he's with you guys.

(Faith crying)

Me to Faith: You okay?

Greg: He's going back to his older son. He's saying that he feels the void that you're feeling. Joe's crying saying he's there when you're in your room alone at night; you wonder and ask if he is there. He says he's there.
 (*Greg laughing*) He says he's a very busy person because he goes from room to room. There is a lot of movement. (*To Nicholas*) He wants you to know that yes he is there and yes, he can hear you. He wants you to know, (Okay, thank you Joe). You've been asking is he is alright and he wants you to know that he is alright. You've been saying "Dad, are you alright?" and he's answering with tears, "Yes, I want you to know that I'm alright."

(Faith softly crying in background)

Greg: Jen, he wants you to know that you're an amazing mom. He says, "Jen! You're an amazing wife and an amazing mother. Never doubt yourself." He's still crying and saying, "Be firm!" and he's using his hand almost like a chopping motion.

Me: Okay. I was firm with Hope because she didn't want to go to bed. I did not want to raise my voice and be firm. I felt a little guilty about it.

Greg: No, don't feel guilty. He says you're very fair. He is saying it again, "You're an amazing mother. You're an amazing Mom!"

Me: Thank you.

Greg: Now he is laughing. He's saying, just follow his lead. He says that the clothes can be laid out the night before, lunches the night before, your son can help out preparing lunches.

Me: These kids have been amazing helping out and they never did anything before. They've been excellent.

Greg: He's laughing and he's saying, "Jen, what you can do is write out a chore list, and they can start on this when they get home from school." He says that everything gets rushed toward the end of the evening and if they have a list of what they know needs to get done…

Me: Yeah it could be kind of a checklist, so I don't have to remind them.

Greg: And laminate it. It could be a star system.

Me: Yes, another thing I have to do. I don't have time for that now.

Greg: No, no, no, not now but, maybe in September when they go back to school.

Faith: I could write it out on my computer.

Me: (To Faith) Oh, that's a great idea. I could write it, and you could type it.

Greg: He's disagreeing with you. He's saying to do it now. Have the kids help out. Each one can take a portion of this. He's coming back to the older one – he can help draft it up, and go to the dollar store to get the stars and all that stuff. He's saying all that can be done now.

Me: Mm-hmm - okay. Yeah like in the summer.

Greg: He's saying sooner than later. To involve them more in this stuff, so you're not taking it all on yourself, or most of it on yourself – you're involving your kids.

Let me see here, ah, something around organizing…

(Me and Faith laughing)

Greg: Okay now, he's telling me something about organizing, something around bath times.

Me: Yeah, Joe used to wash Hope's hair in the shower. Now I'm doing all that.

Greg: He says share that chore because you're going through all that emotional stuff. Give it to one of your older kids to do.

Me: (hesitantly) Okay.

Greg: When you're low in energy to ask them to do that. He's laughing now. Don't just walk away and say 'do that'. You may have to supervise the way its being done.

Faith laughs.

Me: That's very specific.

Greg: No taking shortcuts.

Me: Well, you know, I don't let shortcuts happen.

Greg: That's good. Okay now he's talking about teeth-brushing. "No shortcuts with the teeth-brushing."

Me: I always used to tell him not to let the kids take shortcuts with their teeth brushing.

Greg: He says they should come and show you and smile before they go to bed.

(Nick and Me laugh)

Me: Yes, I sometimes ask them to.

Greg: He's laughing when he says, "You all have great smiles." He's showing me their smiles. It's great.

(Faith giggling in background)

Me to Faith: Do you have any doubt that's your father? That is the most detailed…

Faith: It sounds exactly like him except the organizational part.

Me: It sounds like what I would say from heaven… "Brush your teeth!"

(Greg laughing)

Faith: (humorously) Do your chores kids! Make your bed.

Greg: Ooh, okay. This is for the younger one at bedtime. He wants her to set up her bed like it's a fort. This way nothing bad can get in. And he says it's important, Jen, that you're apart of this; that you're helping to create this around her bed so that 'nothing bad can get in'.

Faith: Dad is acting like a child psychologist now.

Greg: So this way she can feel safe at night.

Me: Well I'm not a good fort builder like he was.

Greg: No, no, no. He's saying you're going to need some string, a flashlight.

Me: I'm not liking the string around them when they sleep. I will do a flashlight.

Greg: He's saying, and I understand your concern, "You're too worried".

Me: I can do pillows. She has a queen bed.

Greg: You can do pillows. You're going to have to organize and tuck her in with the sheets all snug and tight around her so she thinks nothing can get in. The flashlight is in case she feels that she has to turn the light on, so she has it as protection. He's also there as protection.

Me: Mm-hmm.

Greg: And ah, that's it for that. Umm…Let me see what else here…do you guys do story telling at night?

Me: Not really. The kids enjoy reading. They are all good readers.

Greg: He says one thing that would be very helpful is that if you guys had a bedtime story every night, where you're reading to the kids, or the kids can do the reading too.

Me: Yeah we do that at Christmas and Easter – we have our traditional books I read to them, but we could start reading more stories, we have hundreds of books.

Greg: Okay, that's cool. He says get some older person books like Harry Potter.

Faith: Yes I was thinking we should be reading novels.

Greg: Joe was thinking Harry Potter

Faith: That's a good series. It's a bit repetitive but it's good and longer too.

Greg: Yeah, he's saying you could read like a chapter a night.

Me: There you go Faith…

Greg: Does anybody have any questions or anything?

Me: Let me say goodnight to Faith. (Love you, I'll be up to kiss you goodnight).

I have so many questions, and I don't know where to begin. I have so much doubt about how I'm going to manage the house, and am I ever going to feel better? Is it ever going to get easier? I'm getting scared and panicky now.

Greg: What are you getting scared and panicky about?

Me: Things are getting complicated. I'm overwhelmed by how much there is to do. I feel I've got to be him and me. Things were not easy with two of us, with 3 kids and a house. Like the pool house, I want to get it finished. I want to tackle things but I'm afraid to, well right now I'm not ready to, but I'm afraid to ask.

Greg: Is there anyone who could help?

Me: I'm not sure who to ask.

Greg: He's saying that you could appoint your Dad the foreman. Your Dad can oversee it being done. He does not have to do the work himself. He can coordinate with others when they have time and how things will be laid out and getting it done.

Me: It's still early but my Dad made mention of it on the weekend. He understood.

Greg: Appoint him and he'll run with it. He'll figure out what's realistic. Don't worry about any of that.

Joe is saying with emotion, "It's important that you don't go into this thinking that you need to get into both roles, and everything is on you, its okay that you don't have the energy." He's showing me you kneeling on the floor where you have all of your energy completely depleted. He does not want to see you like that. You're far too special. This is where you really need to listen to your intuition. Be in tune with your intuition, because you really are wrestling with a lot. The chores and paperwork aside; going through what you're going though where Joe is, is like 100 jobs in itself, and you really need to take care of yourself. I know you know that but you've got to intellectualize that. Logically you have to integrate that.

Thanks Joe, okay. You're feeling guilty and you feel like you need to take on more than you can, and that's not cool. And there is nothing wrong with having others step in to help out. With your kids it teaches them responsibility, self-respect. It helps them boost their self-esteem and their confidence, and its going to help them in life.

Me: I feel guilty that my daughter is doing dishes. I hated it when I was growing up. I did not have to do them when I was twelve, I hated chores.

Greg: Every situation is different.

Me: All I want is my kids to be good students. That was basically expected of me. I mean my kids are good students.

Greg: They are going to continue with all that stuff but this helps with that too. (Okay, okay Joe). I'm not sure if they are getting allowance but if they're not you might want to start giving them allowance; if they are getting allowance to increase it. That will help too.

Me: What about the big jobs: there are floors, bathrooms and dusting. This is a big house for any couple.

Greg: They need to help out with that also. Include that and rotate the chores. (Okay, thanks Joe) He's saying let them pick and choose what chores they want to do at first. Then there are going to be things that no one wants to do, like scrubbing toilets.

Me: (interrupting) I've had to go out to the dollar store and buy products like toilet brushes. I tackled the toilets.

Greg: He's laughing as you're saying this by the way.

Me: Should I hire a cleaning lady though, a maid?

Greg: If you can afford one, then, for sure. Then again the kids can help out as well. He's saying they need to be responsible for keeping their rooms clean. But with the other chores they can rotate. Is there three floors? I'm getting 3 floors.

Me: Yes, we have a finished basement.

Greg: He's saying they don't all have to be done at once. Focus on a floor at a time. And Joe is saying not to let them cut corners, because Nicholas might say 'I'll do it later, I'm meeting a friend.' Joe's shaking his finger saying, 'No, no, no, no, no, do it before you go out. Be firm that way too.'

Me: I'm worried about Nicholas with school, homework and work. He's a busy boy.

Greg: Well Joe seems to think he can handle it. He has a better idea, I don't know why Joe is saying be prepared for a period where Nicholas will try to get away with stuff. Joe is saying you will be victorious as long as you hold your ground and to remind him in those moments that, 'We're a family; we all need to work together'. This is not the ideal situation and what I would like either, but we all have to do this together.

He's going on about another thing now-Dinners! He's saying its important that everyone helps out and pitches in with dinner and that you all have dinner together every night where possible.

Me: Yeah, it's also what to eat. I don't feel like cooking or eating anymore. I'm just doing it for the kids. I hope I feel better about that, about food…

Greg: Oh, no. You will. Everything you're saying is completely normal. This is not coming from Joe. It's coming from me, because of what I've helped others with before. It's very normal and it is expected. But yes, it will get better. One never forgets anything and nor should anyone, but it does get easier…not to feel guilty about that also. You'll notice when you look back over a period of time how things have changed. Right now, it's literally like moment to moment. Then it's like hour to hour, then its half day to half day, then literally it's day to day.

Me: What does he think of the book idea we had last night? We need his cooperation (laughing).

Greg: He's right on board with it. He thinks it's a great idea, he likes it.

Me: Does he have any psychic ability with the future?

Greg: So he's in a place where, you know the CN Tower? While, on Earth, we're all on the sidewalk, and he's in a place at the top of the space deck of the CN Tower. So in terms of the future, he can see much further ahead than we can. On the sidewalk, we can see only a couple of blocks in front of us; he can see a lot further from his vantage point.

Me: What does he see?

Greg: Good things.

Me: What about in terms of my life purpose?

Greg: Let me see here...Well for one, you're already living your life's purpose. You've got three legacies that you're looking after, number one... (*Greg laughing*), and Joe says, "And mine too!!"

The other thing is your outlook, because of what you're going through others would just lash out at the world and just hate everybody and everything, and complain; and it's so easy to complain anyway, right? When one is going through what you're going through it makes it easy to complain on everything and everybody.

You're not like that at all! Even now, in your darkest hour, you still want to help the world. That's a rarity and that's strength, and Joe's emotional as I'm saying this. This is a strength that you have, that you take for granted. But you think its no big deal, 'it's just the way I am'. But that's not true. It's a huge strength. And it's this strength, coupled with the honest and sincere, and loving person that you are that is going to catapult you forward.

Me: Forward to where? Does he know?

Greg: Forward in terms of helping others and whatever it is that you want to be doing.

Me: I'm not a total saint. I want to be more successful than this.

Greg: You already are, you are just at home, than with others at the moment, but that's where you're needed right now.

Me: Yeah, but I just want to be, like….

Greg: Okay, Joe says, "Slow down - don't rush, you're always in a rush. You're always thinking that you've got to be doing a hundred things at once," and he's telling you, "No, slow down, you don't have to do ten things at once." He's saying the same things now. Right now you've got to put your energy and focus on self-healing, and keeping your family together. He's still emotional and he says "This is what is most important right now." Give that love, nurturing, that caring to yourself and to your family.

So you, for example going out today, to that Rainbow Healing, that's very good, because that's what you need. (Okay thanks Joe!). He's saying "When you're sitting by yourself outside, don't feel guilty for that." He's laughing saying, "If anybody see's you outside, and says, 'Wow, Jen looks so calm and so serene and its good that she's doing that…" He says, "If you could see inside of her mind, it's racing a thousand miles an hour."

Me: Oh, Yeah, right, I always used to sit outside when he was around, but yeah my mind was racing.

Greg: He says, "You've got to work on slowing your mind." That's a big task. Your task is to slow your mind, so you're not feeling guilty that you're taking time for you. What you're working on right now is huge and you need to honour that, and its not that you need to explain this to others, but he says, "Not to worry what others are thinking if they see you taking time for yourself." He's saying that you're worried and thinking that if others see you taking time for yourself that others will say that there are things that need to get done and they're going to think less of you. That's not the case. "Even if that was the case, that's none of their f'ing business."

What is really important is that you take the time for you right now, and it's really important to pull back instead of feeling like you've got to get all these different things accomplished; those should all be secondary. You working on yourself is first and foremost, and whatever you can get done above and beyond that is just an added bonus, okay? And again he's going back to, "You're an amazing mom and amazing mother." He knows that you believe that, but *you* really have to believe that. He doesn't want you second guessing that.

Me: Is my health going to be okay? Will I be better?

Greg: Absolutely. But you have really got to take care of yourself. You're burning your candle out at like 50,000 ends.

Me: Um-hmm. I need my health.

Greg: That's what's causing a lot of the distress within yourself.

Me: Um-hmm, Okay.

Greg: (Thanks Joe). Joe's saying that don't think you have to sit down and have a big meal, full lunch or dinner. With what you're going through, do a lot of snacking, with healthy things, like cheese…he's saying you like cheese?

Me: (Laughing) A little bit, yeah, doesn't everybody?

Greg: Okay, but some people like cheese more than other people.

Me: Well, I have not been eating it, because it's kind of strong. Yes, I used to snack on cheese on a regular basis, before.

Greg: He's saying pick some up, get what you like, especially now. When we're under stress we don't eat as properly as we should. Get your favourite healthy snacks and have those.

He's saying something else here…I just want to hear what he was saying… (Pause)….ooh oh, okay, "You've got to drink more water."

Me: I used to drink a lot but I haven't been. I've been dry.

Greg: He wants you to start doing that again. Even if you carry a bottle around….and you can squeeze some lemon into it (laughs).

Me: Boy, he has a lot of advice. He never had so much advice before. I would cope and do my own thing with common sense, and I had better self-care than he ever did.

Greg: It's a bit of a role reversal.

Me: Will I start sleeping better?

Greg: Yes, you will definitely start sleeping better. He's saying you're feeling like you have to take the meds because you have to be up with the kids and have appointments in the morning. He's saying that if you do not get a good night's sleep that it's okay because once the kids are off you can have a nap. He says not to feel guilty for that. On the other side, there is no time and there is no space. Time is something invented by people. Time is important in the morning with the kids and school. Once they are gone, you don't have time commitments.

Me: For now, yeah.

Greg: He's saying don't take sleeping meds for now and let your body dictate what it needs.

Me: I'm not happy when I'm awake. I'm kind of a night owl but that's okay when you're happy. Now that I'm miserable, I just want to shut down completely.

Greg: There needs to be balance with that too. Don't ignore those feelings completely. Every emotion we're feeling, (this is aside from Joe for a moment, he's listening in), we're taught it's good to feel happy and joy, and when we're feeling like crap we should shelve and hide it away, but those feelings are also important and should be heard.

Me: Yeah, but mine are so intense. Will I be calmer than I was when he was around?

Greg: Oh yeah.

Me: I feel more emotionally calm. I am not crying as much, not shouting. I'm sorry but I feel like he was, uh, the cause of it.

Greg: You think he was the cause of your yelling and stuff?

Me: Yeah, he was really frustrating. I am naturally pretty level headed, except around him.

Greg: He agrees. Uh, yeah he gave you a run for your money.

Me: Yeah, no kidding…he still is.

Greg: He's saying, and he's smiling. He would always do the stuff he preferred to do and the stuff he did not like, he just wouldn't do. He's sad and he knows and he feels badly now that he didn't do the stuff he should have. He's saying one of the things he really enjoyed doing was spending time with the kids.

Me: I used to kind of resent it because I did not have time with the kids.

Greg: He said he used to use it as an escape.

Me: That's okay. I just hope I'll be okay.

Greg: It takes time. He's saying that he has already noticed a difference with you now as opposed to when things just started. Obviously things are not good now but they are better than when he first passed. He's getting sad and emotional. He says he wants you to feel better. He does not like seeing you lethargic, or whatever.

Me: Okay. I think I'll say good night.

Greg: You're okay?

Me: Yeah (sigh) I think he would go all night (laughing).

Greg: He would.

Jennifer Angelee

Me: Can he say one thing of hope or heaven that's not so practical?

Greg: What do you mean?

Me: My life is so gross. It makes me sick. Is there something for the dreamer in me?

Greg: He's saying just be in nature. Do you write poetry?

Me: I wrote a poem today. It came to me in the shower. I jotted it down in a few minutes. It was about him, and it was very deep.

Greg: He's emotional about that. He's saying go to the park everyday if you can and bring stuff where you can do writing with that.
   Do you do sketching too? I'm also seeing that you use charcoal and you do drawing?

Me: I don't but my daughters do. My older daughter is more of an artist.

Greg: Okay thanks Joe, oh. He's saying she can do that while you're writing. Draw the sky or the grass. Interesting, he's showing me more grass than trees.

Me: There is a valley park Joe used to like by the cemetery, and there is a park which I like because it's near water.

Greg: When you can, go to the one where there is water, depending on your mood. He doesn't want you to feel guilty if you don't go where he is buried.

Me: I don't. I can't go. It makes me sick. I don't want the reminder. Talking to him right now, it makes me feel like I'm talking to him on the phone, its okay. It feels energetically like he's still here. I don't feel all alone. It's weird because I used to leave the light on at night when he went to work, and now I just turn all the lights off. It's weird, I just feel safer in my house.

Greg: That's really good.

Me: I feel he is home, in a sense.

Greg: He is, just not in a body.

Me: Unfortunately, yeah he just can't do anything but his mindset is more productive and healthier than before where there would be struggles. It sucks, I constantly say, 'I could have used his help here', 'I could have used his help there', constantly. I feel like I can never turn off. It's a huge adjustment. (Greg listening) Anyway, thanks for being a wonderful medium.

Greg: Thanks for the opportunity.

Me: Thanks. I'm speechless. You're incredible to bring such clarity, for my kids to hear it. It was hard for them but good for them. They needed to hear it. If I could just get a good night sleep tonight and not be so depressed about it. But I guess I can call him when I want, right? I can call him in my head.

Greg: Oh yeah, he'll be with you tonight. He'll be with you the whole night, and he was last night. Even if you need your space and don't want him to be there, he's okay with that. He'll leave you alone. He's sticking very close to you and the kids.

Me: I still cannot believe that I'm talking to him like this. I feel so young to be going through this. I mean I look in the mirror and think I don't look like an old widow.

Greg: (*Laughs*).

Me: (*Joking*) I say look at what he's missing. Unfortunately you can't touch this and I just dropped ten pounds and I still got it.

Greg: You never lost it.

Me: It's just that I don't have a partner to match it. His friend Paul says Joe reminds him of Henry Ford, and everyone thought he would live to 130 but he died of a heart attack at 46.

Greg: That's the thing, we never know.

Me: But it's such an unnatural way to go. It's not meant to be. That's the hard part. That's what upsets me. It might be easier if it were cancer or something.

Greg: That's always hard.

Me: God give me strength. It's unbelievable, unbelievable.

    That night I went to bed alone. I felt the loneliness in my dark room without my beloved husband. How I longed to hold him. Despite the fact that Joe wanted me to sleep with his shirt, these clothes that were so close to his body were just painful, visceral reminders of what I was missing. It took me almost two years to feel some comfort wearing his night t-shirts and pajama bottoms to bed. The nights were often long and sleepless, and waking to the realization of my new life without Joe were the most dreadful moments of my life. Of course, this pain did recede and when I dreamed of Joe, I knew he was with me each morning. I still awoke disappointed by the realization that he is no longer with us in the physical. This is my cross to bear, the price for having found true love while incarnated in a physical body.

Chapter 8

Soft Petals and Angel Wings

"In the night of death, hope sees a star, and listening love can hear the rustle of a wing." ~ Robert G. Ingersoll

Earlier on the day of the reading with Greg on May 27, 2015, I had a Rainbow Healing Session with Chris Cuciurean. I knew Chris Cuciurean as an Angel Healer and I had seen him before my son's kidney transplant. I had also taken Angel Workshops with him, and been to his Mediumship Circles. The Rainbow Energy Healing Session was new to me. I hoped it would help heal my body on a spiritual level.

Immediately, Archangel Michael was found to be at my right side. Also found were different ancestral spirits from both my mother and father's lineages. Chris said that if he was unaware of the circumstances that brought me there that day, it was apparent that I was going through an awakening. He said it is, "The beginning of a very fertile period of growth. The curtain is being drawn; this is the beginning of a new phase of empowerment. The empowerment comes from being righteous, which means being a humble servant of the divine, being congruent with a higher power for guidance and wisdom and direction. You had these challenges before but you carried a lot of this energy in your solar plexus."

Chris continued to read me during the Rainbow Healing session on the table. "It feels like your solar plexus has opened a trap door to allow that divine light to come in from above. In the next couple of years, you're going to go through a transformation. There are two issues around Joe's passing and him being in a different state that are really a blessing. One is that he can be of help without physical distraction and mental energy which is muddied. And the other one is empowering you more effectively. I think he has always been an admirer of you, and he is in a place where he has an opportunity to deal with his own issues. He is in a place where he can support your mission. His idea of surrendering to the divine was not the same as yours when he was here. He is saying, 'You go girl' with blessing. His wish for you becomes more amplified where he is. The wanting to see you succeed and do well can be done more effectively where he is at. I don't know if he can see that yet."

"I have Archangel Chamuel showing me your heart chakra. Your heart chakra is huge, it's almost swollen. We are balancing the chakras; there is just so much energy in the heart. What you are experiencing through the heart is intense, you must be on overload."

I replied, "I feel like I have such heartache."

"It's vulnerable, swollen; we are going to tighten it up and were going to bring it back to a normal size. It's full of over-inflated emotion. We need to fill your heart with your energy. It's got everyone else's in there. It's starting to push away the dark cloudy greys. Chamuel has the most amazing whitish pink light and he is healing your heart."

"I have Mother Mary here. Master Jesus is kneeling before you at the table. He's on the right side holding your hand. He's saying that the divine father has willed it to be so, you are safe. You are in divine salvation under the watch and protection of the divine father. That is what the two of them are representing here. Mother Mary is on your left side. Jesus is holding your right hand and saying 'I pray to the Father'. This is very much God the Father Energy. Mother Mary is the divine goddess, she is the nurturer, and you were conceived in love before time began. She models that so well for us."

"The heart has really calmed down. It's gone back into proportion to the other chakras. The heart and solar plexus chakras are in competition. Lead with the heart....There is a lot of gold energy which tells me the ideas you have about yourself are being protected."

"I feel like a dripping yellow fluid coming out of my solar plexus."

"Your mental body is so huge and swollen also. It's consumed with thoughts: *What am I going to do? How am I going to do this?* Your solar plexus needs to be cleansed too. There are too many thoughts that aren't serving you, competing for your awareness. I am going to cleanse that with a liquid light yellow…"

"I am moving up to the throat chakra. I am getting the message, 'Keep asking for help'. You keep putting yourself in the martyr role. It's hard, I know, you've been let down by a lot of people who have chosen life paths and very different value systems. In familial and business relationships, you've been let down by people who have not made the most noble choices, and you have this sense that you need to control things through your solar plexus. Your throat needs to start saying out loud, 'This is my vision', and so people can figure out how they can help. You have a lot of great thoughts in the solar plexus, there are just so many, that it's clogging things up. The best way to express these visions is to say, *"Here is my vision, here is my hope; I am envisioning this happens with supper, or this happens with the girls."*

"The sacral chakra is our emotions and our joys which have been on hold for the last weeks. What it feels like to me is the energy of the inner child. She wants to get attention also. This is where we nurture from. This is going down into the inner child and saying, 'Am I lovable?' The message is around a mother's pride; Mother Mary is here with you, looking on you with pride. You are the creator's beloved joy, the creator's crown achievement."

(Laughing) "Do you say that to everybody?"

"You and I are."

"How often do you say that? The way you said that sounds very special."

"That is the energy of the creator. How often do they say it like that? Not a lot. Sometimes the creator will say, 'You can do better. You need to get your act together'. Everybody gets it differently. The message for you today is the creator wants to pick you up and hold you like a child… when I'm speaking I'm just saying what is popping into my head. Same is with the clairaudience; whatever I say is just coming in the present. To be honest, I have never done a Rainbow Energy Session so soon after someone has lost a loved one like you have. So for me I'm seeing the over-inflation of the heart chakra and the rainbow healing energy is actually calming it down. In the sacral and the heart, I'm witnessing your innocence. To me, it's something to behold but my job here is to be a witness to that energy and report it as I'm guided to. This is for you to cherish and say 'thank you to the creator'. The creator loves you. This is an incident of the higher power loving its creation. There is no doubt about it; you are the pinnacle of the achievement of the creator. You are mindful of how infinite we are to the creator and we are yet, so small, anything is possible, anything is possible…"

"Here comes Archangel Azrael. I see a bunny rabbit hopping through the earth. This is a sign of fertility and abundance. I really do feel like this is an opening, a passageway to something very profound in terms of how you're guided."

"And Archangel Raziel is working on the third eye here, in the pineal gland. His name means 'secrets of God'. He is massaging that area with his thumbs….lots of indigo blue, lots of green, deep healing is happening on a tissue level on the cells of your body, to every fibre of your being. There is rejuvenation happening on behalf of your children, to each of your organs, to your kidneys and liver. Thank you Archangel Raziel. Now he is pulling away from the brain and bowing to the Seraphin, caressing you with feathers. The Seraphin are one of the highest realms of angels. They are like white, silvery gold, holding you in admiration. They are here to serve. There is no lack, there is pure love, pure devotion."

"Moving down to the root chakra…we're clearing around energy that does not need to be held onto…"

"I just got turquoise light under my eyelids. It's so green…, normally its red but I'm seeing green."

"Yeah there's Raphael. It's passing down your spine, into the root."

"It's so cool to see the colours in my eyes."

"Yes, they're showing you the visuals…I'm getting Archangel Cassiel, the angel of tranquillity, tranquillity and peace. The tranquillity that Archangel Cassiel brings is very Atlantean, like an ocean-like Shangri-la. It's very watery, it's very fluid."

"There is some pressure in my forehead."

"There is a lot of activity in your third eye right now. It's like a fire hydrant but its light pouring out, or like fireworks. Its white and silver, that's what's coming out of your third eye. There is definitely a third eye, awakening, clearing happening today, and I'm kind of just in amazement because the timing for me (of you just going into some higher degree of clairvoyance/psychic connection is just amazing, but that's what's happening)."

"Let's just work on some chakras above the crown, starting with your sacred life purpose, and soul contracts."

(Me Interrupting) "I don't want to suffer, that's why I'm ready, I need this (change)".

"As you said that I was at your feet and Archangel Zadkiel came in. Zadkiel is all about compassion and mercy."

"This chakra is usually about the size of a beach ball above the crown and it is swollen. I have never seen it swollen to this degree. There is a lot of thought going into 'how my circumstance affects my life purpose…' You will get back to what you've been doing; you will get back to what you have been doing but with a completely new vantage point. With clarity and with a compassion for self, as well as for all who have suffered….One of the aspects of your life purpose is to be in a position to help those who have silently suffered, who have silently struggled, who haven't had a voice…it feels as if I'm going to go up to a higher chakra which is the soul's purpose, which includes all of your past lives, it's written in the Akashic Field, in the Akashic Records. But it feels like in past lifetimes, your soul simply gathered case studies of women who suffered and it was never known, it was never brought to light and it took courage, and they took their secrets to the grave. I feel like you gathered awareness of this in past lifetimes in order to learn to help, in order to release people from silence, from suffering, and inability to reach out, to reach out and help, and get help."

"I have Archangel Metatron, showing me the energy grids and meridians of your soul group and those here to help. One person who comes to mind is a doctor that worked on your son's case?"

"Yes, my son's rare illness was a medical case study for him that gave us answers, and he wrote a book which included my son's medical story. It was very inspiring to me."

"It's just the beginning. It continues in your journey. You are not meant to know it. It's not coming to me. I see a timeline and I see gaps or patches that I'm not being shown what is going to happen over the next four to five years. I feel like it is divinely meant to occur.

How does it help you? Your mission involves you actually growing and expanding, a higher level of surrender and being guided day to day, a greater use of your third eye and your clairvoyance. There is an awakening of this on Earth. Whether Joe was here or not, this was meant to happen for you. You are going through a continued awakening. Every time I say this stuff, your children's guides come in a wave their hands and say 'we need this to happen', so it has a lot to do with all three of your children."

"So there is a five year time span. It is with your children. I actually see you as a supporter of their mission, and them taking the stage in fifteen years when they are a supporter of you. Their voice, their charisma, their presence, their actions and activities actually open the way for you. But what happens in the next few years, um, first step is you have to integrate the knowledge of this shift for you. This family shift, this dynamic is an important part of your life mission, to suddenly have the perspective change, to have it twisted and turned on you, as a Mom, and as a wife; it is a key element of your path."

"Is it, was it meant to be like this?"

"There are different ways it could have been like this…"

"Ahhh (big sigh), it hurts. It hurts that I have to do it this way. I didn't want to do it without Joe."

"The thing is you're not doing it without him. You're doing it now, with him in a different form."

"But I wanted him in the physical."

"I keep getting 'come back to what I told you five minutes ago'. You help people who have suffered in silence, and you give them a voice. You will experience suffering in this shift, but you won't lose your voice over it. Um, but others have. The actual content of your messages that you deliver to people in ten or fifteen years, you don't know it, you think you're closer than you are, but you don't know it yet. The dynamic is that in past lives is that you gathered the energy of willpower, and determination because you saw people suffer in silence. So it is just something that is unacceptable to you, that some element of creation can be seemingly left behind. So your son's rare illness is but a form of that suffering in silence. Something most people don't have to face. Someone living with sudden loss of a spouse with children, that's silent suffering. Those people shouldn't have to face it alone. There's more, there's more than just those."

"I am thinking of my grandmother that was a single mother."

"It's interesting. There are ancestors with you, cousins and uncles who

Beloved, I Can Show You Heaven

were observers of that dynamic from the perimeter but not in the heart of it."

"I also feel like a connection to northern Europe, to like Ireland, like I was a druid."

"Yeah (inflecting laughter), as soon as you say that, you have ancient guides that are dressed in robes with strange, different proportioned crosses, holding them, and you have a lot of connections to sects, like religious sects, that existed in that time of the druids."

"I'm not even sure when that is…"

"To me the religion is not Christian. It's very pagan. Um, it is very Earth, and worldly aware. It is very aware of the Earth, and the solar system and the stars and systems of the planet. It is a really, really ancient wisdom".

"There is like a fibre optic grid above your head and below your feet, so when we align that grid with yours, and mother earth, we get more empowered with earth energy. We get more grounded, more supported with everything the earth has to offer. Then there's a cosmic grid. When we connect to that, it helps us to connect with higher guidance and higher being."

"There is an energy system to that, and where you fit into the world. If you see where I'm at now, Jen, I'm up here way above your head. There is a chakra, and it's called the Fifteenth, it's very beautiful, and all I'm hearing is that little child in you saying, 'And nobody gets left behind, and nobody gets left behind' and I really feel the really strong passion for inclusion, for everybody to be included and everybody to be worthy of joy, or bliss – an external manifestation of Heaven on Earth. This is really the Heaven on Earth Chakra, and there is just this awareness of your higher self and a being of pure light. There is this really unique snowflake vibration that the creator made. And above this I see this whole team of ancestors and guides, and I'm literally bridging the gap of that Shangri-La World that you want to create where no one gets behind and all the voices of ancestral guides, and past life guides and relationships. So, just know that you don't have all the information you need right now to put into practice what you need to do. You are still in the information gathering phase. I think it involves the next 5-6-7 years of your life fulfilling your divine contract as a mother. This doesn't mean you need to stop being a light worker, a redeemer of faith that we can transcend. So you are that, but it's going to come after, but your oldest, is what, about 13?"

"No, he will be 18 in October."

"Oh, 18, how old is your oldest girl?"

"She's 12."

"Okay, so for me, when the 12 year old girl is 17-18, so that's five to six years. That is the time frame that you've gathered the information as fulfilling the primary function of being a Mom. That's a big part of your life purpose right now, but it transitions into what your children will be doing. It feels like with the girls, what they will be doing at that post high school age, it will then be very clear who your guided to help and how. But in the next few years, you're gathering who has suffered silently in different forms, through illness, you're being helped by so many."

"Do you know Faith's life purpose?"

"Were almost finished here, let's ask that question when were sitting. Right now she's by your womb, and I just see you holding her like a mama bear (laughing)."

"As we're finishing this session here, I just see this image of a large, mother goddess. She's pulling you into her heart centre and embracing you. Divine father, firm, masculine hands upon your crown, granting eternal life. When you know that you are eternal, you will use your physical life and its relationships to its highest potential. Just remember that you are eternal. You cannot be destroyed; as the Creator opens their hands to you in light, as the Christ in me and you, and all beings. Christ exemplified as Jesus, Buddha, and Mother Mary. I see Jesus leading the path for you…There is a golden light that opens up for you in your chest, from the centre of your heart. Jesus is with you, beside you, showing you that Christ is there."

"My throat is scratchy."

"Your own energy is struggling to find the meaning, just speak of your vision, what will unfold for you and your children; just let it be. They are held beautifully in light, they are divine. Sometimes the throat; you want to verbalize control; you're not going to be in control. Your children are reaching their right to independence. Just speak of what you envision, what you hope for. Just keep saying to your children, 'This is what I see…'. They will go away, and ruminate on it and it will come back better than you dreamed. You can see when people are not behaving divinely, just keep saying, 'This is what I envision, what I see as potential', and let everything manifest. Voice ideas as visions, as hope and as possibilities and by stating that, you're inviting them to join in and co-create with you. You don't have to own everything; they will deal with things in each of their own ways, in their own time."

"The solar plexus says, 'We've got to take action, this is how we should behave'. Your throat does not have to say, 'This is what has to happen'. Know that your children are protected and being supported by the divine and by their own higher selves. They will cope, adapt and heal. Your path and your children's are always very tightly coupled. You even have some more tight coupling to go."

"Yeah, we're working together more, whereas before, they were always doing their own thing. I felt like I was losing them a little bit and now we're working together, and cooperating. It's awesome but I don't like the circumstances around it."

"The divinity within them is saying that I have to be there for that family unit."

Chris closed with a prayer. After the Rainbow Healing Session and lying on the table, Chris and I sat in the living room sofas of his healing studio and discussed my questions. He talked about the process of Nicholas incarnating and how with him, it was an especially special process.

Chris began the reading:

Chris: As much as his father' death is sad, it is setting the stage for what he needs to go and do now. His contract in life involves his Dad's life coming to an end.

Me: What about me? It's interesting because I had a reading on April 29th with Carol Righton and she asked me if I was moving. I said I had no plans. She said she saw me building a cottage and writing in front of a lake with pine trees. Now my future is anything could happen. I don't know. Is there anything with that? I can hold onto the house but its so much work now. Joe did everything. I just want to know, 'Where am I going?' Joe was my soul mate. It doesn't get any better than that. I want a partner.

Chris: What I was getting is over the next five years, your primary purpose is parenting but you are still gathering information. That gathering is done by you alone, not as a soul mate relationship. You're getting in touch with all that you've learned, all that you've gathered; you're going to be working on a mission. You're very driven. I see lots of handwriting and pen writing. I see you as an author, penning journals and books. This is part of information gathering. It's putting out statements and getting feedback... For example, 'oh someone was helped by that' or 'someone can relate to that'. Writing is very good for you. In terms of a partner, I'm going to ask now...

The relationship is not based on who you are today. It is based on who you are five, six, seven years down the road. You take what you are building in terms of greater self-awareness and this is what I'm putting out there in terms of building that partnership. Right now, you don't know what you're putting out there because there is a phase of un-building the karma of you being you and Joe. You have carried his karmic baggage. He had a lot of karmic baggage, and he is going to process that in spirit and he is going to help you process yours. He is going to be better equipped energetically to help you process and hold light and prayers for you, and to call in support from other heavenly beings, and to watch over you and perform small miracles, on behalf of the divine, on your behalf so you can deal with your karma, your baggage, your issues. Those issues that you deal with will make you into a different person than you are today. That person that you attract in three, four, five, six years is different than who you are today, in terms of a possible partner.

So my sense is that you will not be granted a partner in terms of a long term partner. You will have people who come in who are known as Arcs whose paths cross with yours.

Me: Will they be like boyfriends?

Chris: Yes, to me there is a physical closeness, and yet they're...

Me: It's hard to imagine myself in a new marriage commitment.

Chris: Yes, so right now you have your children. You and your children as a team and there is arms length around that, and I don't see you saying you're going to invite a new fifth member to the team. It's going to take you some time to say the four of us are a team, and for you as an individual to team with one person. The person may have their own children, and be aware of your family dynamic, but is not merged with it. They are not congruent with it. Your life path and all the other things you're going to do with your children, it doesn't feel like you're ready. What it feels to me is like is a need for affection, that closeness, and that will come as divine merciful blessings, like people who come in. They come in, and they transition and they go where they need to go, because they were not meant to go together forever. The person you're meant to meet has to be after you have integrated the knowledge of what you and Joe were, and you have not begun to grasp it. You will grasp it over time. You're going to take that time to go 'Hmm, that's what that was. I never really thought of it this way'. You're going to go through different stages of that, and that will allow you to say, 'That was who I was. Look at what I have become.' And when you put, 'Look at what I've become' out to the world, it's not someone who is temporarily crossing paths with you.

It looks to me like you're a lighthouse, and these other being are like rays of light. They can't get attracted to you now, because you don't have the right vibrations to match that now. The lighthouse and rays are not beaming close enough and are missing each other because neither of you are at the right vibration to match in a relationship. I know it's kind of a weird metaphor, but the two of you are on opposite shores right now. The two of you are beginning to grow, and the growth involves looking forward, than looking back right now."

Me: Um-hmm. It's hard. It's so scary.

Chris: It is…

Me: Joe and I had a perfect physical attraction. We had a perfect, instant attraction. But we had that kind of relationship where it was either wonderful, or it was terrible. I miss that physical relationship the most, and being without that, scares me the most.

Chris: Think of it as being a contract as souls, who are not physical, who had a contract to be together for a set of milestones which were completed.

Now think of it that you are in a period of growth, for yourself, and further self-discovery, so you can re-create that again. You can re-create that perfection again, but it's going to be a different version of you than what it was than when you met Joe.

Me: Oh yeah, Jen 2.0. I was only 18, yeah.

Chris: Jen 2.0, huh. That's a good way to say it, because it feels…It's just amazing, you're starting a brand new phase…

Me: Am I going to miss that?

Chris: You're going to miss that. I can feel it already, and I have tears and emotion coming. There is going to be emotional responses to the lack of that physical presence… There is a lot of learning, letting go, and being the Jen that has to compensate for Joe's lack, and becomes self-sustaining, and becomes independent. You're going to go through that. I went through that (divorce) and when I look back, I realize I had to do that alone. You didn't choose this, but you are going to face it head on. You are a determined soul, and so you will find your way through it. However, you will miss someone to kiss, someone to hold, someone to snuggle with, or even pick up a grocery bag, or hold a door. You will miss that.

Me: I miss that for my kids. It pains me, like going to soccer…my kids don't have a Dad.

Chris: It's more adapting to doing what you can alone, and your kids adapting. You can try different things. You don't always have to be the one with the answer. The creator knows you're not expected to be a handyman and everything you and Joe did together. Your children know that. There is a period of adaptation.

When I went through it, it allowed me to discover parts of myself that I had masked or repressed because she didn't need it or want it. I was doing things I did not want to do because I was doing it to compensate for her baggage or karma, or lack. When the relationship ends, you have to let go and find there is more to you than meets the eye right now.

When you look down the road, you're going to realize that there is so much that you've learned about yourself. And that is the person that you are going to put out there to attract. Who that is, is so much more, more in-depth, and more well-rounded. There is someone out there who is going to be more attracted, who is deeper, already more self-aware than you are now.

You're going to go through a phase, and then there will be that new relationship.

Me: Will I feel that attraction, though? Because I was so attracted to Joe.

Chris: Yes, for sure. You have so many souls in your soul group to repair the passageway, activating healing. You will come across a lot of people where there is an instant chemistry. You may come across people who feel it with you, and you don't and vice-versa. It's a blessing to feel that, to go out on a date. It doesn't feel like the time is critical, it's the stages of growth, where you are okay to be in touch with another human being, even if it is not thee person. It will serve a temporal purpose.

Chris explained the energy grid in my aura and how they were worked on during the healing session to become light activated. He explained how these energy centres are creating stronger attractions and connections. If people are not connected by my life purpose and the light, they literally will start to fall away. Chris stated, "Don't be surprised if you meet someone and there is a connection that feels familiar. You may not know what the purpose of the relationship is. You'll wonder what's there; maybe you're there to help each other."

Me: I feel I've been given back to myself, but was it necessary for me to have such profound loss?

Chris: Honestly, there is not a 'had to be that way'. It's sudden and profound, but it's not going to serve you to say, 'Does it have to be this way?' What will serve you better is, 'It is this way, and how am I going to deal with it? I'm going to call on my higher power'. If you need to ask for help, you're doing so many of the right things so rapidly, that going into that analysis is going to derail you. It's going to clog you up, instead of allowing the blessings to unfold. You're getting a lot of blessings from the community, and people want to help you. And your children are capable of stepping up, and they know it. They will deal with the grief. Grief is a form of love that will show them how much they love their father. You can tell them, 'Its okay to cry and to miss him because it's your way of showing everyone that you really loved Dad.'

Me: I feel his death was accidental. In some ways he didn't think he would succeed, there was hesitation and it was too late.

Chris: From what I got in the session is he is very much cocooned. His energy is off to the right side, and I feel like the joy of getting to heaven he wants to share with you. He looks at you with tremendous reverence because of your faith and perseverance. There's a real deep sense of amazement over you, but there is also dealing with the feeling of, *'Gosh, if I could turn back time. Gosh, what have I done???'*

We all experience a level of 'Ugh! Jeez, I wish I didn't do that.' He's experiencing that at a profound level right now, and he needs time to cope with that. The type of reading you will get from him down the road will be different because he will have had time to process and gather a lot of insight.

Me: Am I picking up on his regret?

Chris: Yes, for sure. Your heart that was really swollen, that was literally him clinging to you too. He also needs to grieve. He has a consciousness.

Me: He said he climbs into bed with me. I felt him this morning, but then it was too much...

Chris: It is too much. You have to separate that energy. There are some times when you'll have to say, 'I need to spend tonight alone', and there will be times you'll say, 'I'm glad you're with me, but I need to get used to this Joe.' There is a give and take, like you said there are times when it's wonderful and times when its terrible, its not that he needs to be your energetic companion for 24 hours. You need your space; you need to find in it in you how you deal with how to be a single Mom. You're not a single Mom like a divorced single Mom. You are a Mom of three children with a loving father who has passed. That's a little different, energetically that can be a good thing. So when you're dealing with crisis you can say, 'Joe, I need your help!' You can literally say that and you'll see some magic happen. My sense is that in three months and six months, you will see different quality and growth from him, because he is still perceiving time, and he is still experiencing what's happened, and that's typical. He took everything with him, except the physical vessel, so he just doesn't have a physical body to express with, but he still has all the emotions and all the thoughts, and the mind racing to get caught up in all the 'what ifs', and can say, 'Who am I relation to God?'

Joe's dealing with a lot in himself, and there are times when you need to say, 'I need to be alone.' Like how you said what you needed today, he did not impose his will to come through, and I've seen spouses who have passed do that, and they are a little bit pushy. He's very respectful, very mindful, very aware. He's been made very aware, 'Here's what's going on, on the earth plane', and there's a tremendous amount of remorse, but also a tremendous amount of 'I wanna help..., what can I do?' so you can ask for what you want, but you can also ask for your space.

Me: Sometimes when I feel him around the most, is when it's the most painful. Like in the car from the soccer game, I missed him more. It's awful; I've never felt anything so bad in my entire life.

Chris: Like I said with the kids, that grief is a form of love too. The depth of grief is the depth of love. If you can realize that grief is just the profoundness of the love you're experiencing.

Chapter 9

The Thorn and the Roses

"My love for you will outlast this beach, this ocean, this planet. When judgement comes and Heaven finally falls, I will take you back with me." - Scarlett Blackwell, I Am Fallen

Greg the Medium became a friend during those first weeks of grieving Joe. By the beginning of June, only weeks after Joe's death, I was in the depths of despair. Joe had not yet crossed into the fullness that Heaven has to offer. He had come back and rarely left my side. I know he was still tortured and carried the pain of regret. Picking up on Joe's emotion meant that energetically I was not only grieving his loss, I was carrying the burden of his emotion as well.

Joe attached to Greg and used him as a medium to help me. Greg inadvertently had become a facilitator to Joe and I communicating. Greg rescued me many times from total despair as Joe was like a lassie dog barking that I had fallen into a well. As crazy as it seems, Joe made a habit of disturbing Greg at his work to aid me. Joe would show up while Greg was at work in his office so that he would call me.

When I was at home in the mornings after the kids had gone to school, I was depressed and clinging to life most days. Greg would call me. I'd answer the phone from bed. Greg would say, "Jen, what are you doing right now?" I would cry and Greg would reassure me, "Jen, you're going to be okay. Put your feet on the floor, go downstairs and have coffee and eat breakfast." I would explain how I felt so miserable I was too nauseous to eat, my coffee would make me vomit, I was dizzy…

All of it was true. I lost weight so quickly, eating became torture. I couldn't stomach the idea that Joe was gone; all pleasure in eating seemed forever lost. Food tasted gross! My skinny clothes that I never thought I'd fit into became loose. Greg patiently coaxed me by telling me he wouldn't talk to me unless I ate something. Desperate to communicate with him and Joe, I would try so hard, but all I really wanted to do was crawl into a ball and have God take me to the other side.

I remember one particular morning I was desperately anxious and deeply depressed. Greg was at work and he had his phone off when I called him. Joe literally showed up at his work.

"Call her!" Joe said.

Greg replied, "I can't, I'm in a meeting right now."

Persistently Joe continued, "Call her, call her, call her!"

Greg responded, "I am in a meeting, I cannot, I will call her on my break."

Joe said, "Well, when is that?"

Greg told him he wasn't sure but Joe continued stubbornly, not giving up.

"Fine," Greg said to Joe as he raised his hand in the meeting, "I would like to know what time we get a break?"

He continued, feeling silly, "I need to get a drink at that time."

"Okay" the managing presenter said, "We will take a break at 10:45. Is that okay with you?"

Satisfied, Greg said to Joe, "I will call her at 10:45, okay?" Joe agreed and Greg called me at that earliest opportunity concerned for me. He told me the antics Joe had put him up to. It's a funny and sad story at the same time, but it gave me comfort at the lengths Joe would go to reach out to me in my need.

Greg and I spent many nights on the phone, sometimes a bit too late into the night after the kids had gone to bed talking about Joe's death and the emotions I was going through. I had many deep burning questions about the afterlife with suicide, why this happened, and where my life was going. I was desperate for reassurance. I was working through practical issues of survival and at the same time, the state of my soul and Joe's.

I remember one evening Greg and I were talking and Joe abruptly entered Greg's apartment bedroom. Greg asked me if I heard the biggest thump. I didn't, but Joe arrived like a superhero, shaking his mirrored closet doors. Greg told me it was really cool. He said he liked Joe's energy and he was very cool. He never seemed to mind Joe's intrusion into his life. As Greg and I talked, Joe was often on the phone listening to our conversation. Greg often said, "He's here, he's listening to us" or "He is nodding his head in agreement." Sometimes Joe would intercept Greg's talking and throw his two cents in. He even intercepted text messages between Greg and me, adding emoticons of kissy-faces from Joe to me. Greg and I found these quirks amusing, and he would point out the unusual things that Joe had caused.

Greg came over one evening in July, 2015 and he read Joe for me with our intention to learn things to put this book together. Greg and I sat in my family room on sofa's facing across from each other. Before we sat and relaxed, I mused to Greg how I had wished I could get the beautiful pool lights working in the pool like Joe always had. I was so frustrated with the situation. I missed sitting around the pool on summer nights with the beautiful, serene pool lit in aqua green. As Greg and I began by conversing on the couches, we discussed issues just six weeks after Joe's crossing:

Greg: He's saying he has these feelings where he yearns to be with you, and he knows he cannot be with you. There is a lot of emotion as I'm saying this: "He's reaching his arms out, he's doing this (hugging motion), and he is saying that while there is other stuff to discuss, he doesn't want you to feel guilty, or have remorse, he's not blaming…he wants to clear the air on everything, or some things."

I explained that I was the only one close to hold him besides the kids, so when I miss him, it is the most intense.

Greg: It's interesting…he says that no matter how many miles he drives, he is still a million miles away from you. It's an interesting analogy. No matter if he drives 40,000 miles, he is still that much further away from you. So no matter what he tries to do, he will never get there.

Beloved, I Can Show You Heaven

Me: Will he ever be able to get closer to me physically? In my dreams?

Greg: Not for awhile… because when you wake up the next morning, it's going to be that much harder, he doesn't want that. He's trying to be cognizant of that too. He wants you to know he's around, but he doesn't want it to be so intense that when you wake up you say to yourself, "Oh shoot, here I am again."

Me: How come I can't see him in the physical?

Greg: (laughing) He's laughing, he says that he would freak the hell out of you if he did that. He said you'd be totally freaked out and that is not the purpose of that. So he comes to you in ways that you'll be okay with.

Me: Yeah, because I may not be able to get back to sleep, in like forever (laughs).

Greg: Exactly. (Listening to Joe, long pause) He's saying now that you are obviously aware that he was a workaholic who kept himself busy all the time. He is using the word exhausted, he had trouble sleeping, was restless…

Me: He didn't structure his downtime.

Greg: He's saying he's worried and concerned for you too. He's upset and saying that life is too short to be running around and worrying about all the different things that you worry about on a daily basis. He says it's so insignificant, just slow down. It's important to slow down, stop, and look around and just 'be' once in a while.

Me: (Crying) I can understand why he would be worried about me because now I'm doing the jobs of both of us and dealing with my grief, and I already had health problems to begin with. I feel like I have no choice. Everyone is getting on my case. I would like to breathe, but I feel like I have not been able to breathe since he left (crying). Every morning I wake up I wonder if I'm ever going to get a true, psychological break again. I don't have anyone else to rely on. Like last night it was 10:30 when I realized that no one reminded me to dry the kid's bed sheets I had washed. They needed to go to bed and they didn't have bedding on their beds. I was exhausted.

Greg: And that's what Joe means by not sweating the small stuff.

Me: And I always have a sore back. The small stuff does get me worked up because it is a big deal for me to figure things out. Everything is a challenge, on the other side you can make things happen with the speed of thought. But not having the things I want easily manifest, makes me miss Joe more.

Greg: But Jen – your health is incredibly important, for you Jen; not for anybody else.

Me: (Crying) There is not that little bit of time at the end of the day to chill out with someone. Before, even if Joe was going to work, I could go to bed and relax, and now I cannot sleep. I had to spend two hours with the lawyer today, that sucked. It doesn't feel like I have a moment.

It's just really hard to relax right now into my life. Joe was always the light at the end of the tunnel. I'm sad that he couldn't relax with me. I think he had a hard time relaxing, period. Like on vacation, he couldn't relax. He could not relax, even when he had an opportunity.

Greg: Why was that?

Me: I think that is when depression set in. He didn't do what he did because of this, did he?

Greg: He's saying he felt overwhelmed. It was too much. (Long pause, deep sigh) He says he didn't try talking to you about this because you're such a strong woman.

Me: What does that have to do with it?

Greg: Umm, I don't even know how much you're aware of your strength.

Me: Everyone always says, 'You're so strong and stuff...'

Greg: Yeah! You're strong! It's good but at the same time…

Me: Does he mean I'm powerful?

Greg: Yeah! So like when you're firm on something, you're firm on something. No one is going to shake you from that.

Me: This is my fault then….?

Greg: It's not your fault, because he didn't say anything. Any relationship, these things do come up but with different things. It's important that we're able to talk about it. Part of the reason he was here in the physical is to be able to voice himself.

Me: When Joe was young, he was a bit of a maniac. He worked so hard and was go, go, go. After he donated his kidney, he seemed to slow down, was what happened because he donated a kidney?

Greg: (long pause listening). He's saying when he had the kidney transplant, it changed his perspective on life, and it's sad because I asked him if he shared this with Jen, and he said, 'Well no.' and that's sad because it's such an important and touching thing and it was such an epiphany for him. He's saying that at the time, he didn't think you would be open to it, and now in hindsight he thinks that maybe you would have.

Me: What was the epiphany? Did the kidney transplant physically slow him down?

Greg: No, no, no. The epiphany was that life is too short and not to sweat the small stuff.

Me: Yeah, he didn't share that with me at all, because he never even told me to not sweat the small stuff.

Greg: He just said he never told you that.

Me: I would have appreciated if he communicated with me not to sweat the small stuff. When we lost Joseph, I felt like he was always on the go, and he took for granted we were going to have another baby. I thought that was a wake up call for him. Before, we had Nicholas he was so driven, such a workaholic, I could never pin him down. The kids made him more aware. He had a lot more time than I did to play with the kids. If I knew he was thinking, 'life was too short' maybe I would have done differently. He never told me to slow down.

Many times I worked just as hard, or harder, but people didn't see it. He didn't appreciate it. He left just as it was getting easier. This summer we could have relaxed. This summer he just put it all on me and now I can't relax. Doesn't he know that? That's the truth.

Greg: Well, when he did that, he wasn't thinking at all, he wasn't thinking about the future.

Me: I guess he wasn't thinking about that when he did what he did. It was a permanent solution to a temporary problem.

Greg: He wasn't thinking at all in that moment and as soon as he did it he realized and said, 'Oh shit.'

Me: Does he feel guilty? Guilty about the kids?

Greg: Oh yeah, he feels a lot of remorse Jen! Absolutely! He feels like shit! Those are his words.

Me: Shittier than I feel?

Greg: Oh yeah.

Me: Physically or emotionally?

Greg: Emotionally because he doesn't have a body. Again, he had all those emotions he had to work through and then in addition to that, he has what he's done to work through, and what he's done to all of you here, as well as your families and friends, that he has to deal with. It's a lot; he's not off scot-free at all. He has to come back to work on that again.

Me: Can he help us?

Greg: Your lives are moving forward and it's going to get easier. He's helping as much as he can.

Me: Can he make things happen? Like with synchronicity?

Greg: What do you mean by that?

Me: Like Nicholas getting into College or Faith a Scholarship…

Greg: Oh, yeah, yeah, yeah. What he just showed me is each of them sitting in a push car and he's there behind, pushing them. He just gave me that analogy. He's totally there for them, always.

Me: Like, opportunities might come up that would not be possible if he were here in the physical… Like Faith can wish for a particular scholarship but he will wish on the same star with her?

Greg: He's laughing he's saying they have to put the work in, and he will give it a push like with each of them driving each of their own cars.

Me: What about me?

Greg: (Laughing) He's laughing right now, he's saying he's going to give you a kick in the butt. (Laughing) He says he's going to kick your ass. He's joking, laughing.
   No, no, seriously, of course he's there for you too. He doesn't want anything more than your happiness.

Me: Is he going to give me luck with work or my career or my book?

Greg: This is where you have to do the soul searching. He can't make choices for you. Once you're a thousand percent sure of what you want to do, yes, he will help you with that. He's not going to tell you what to do.

Me: So he won't make things happen that may or may not be good for me because everything has a price.

Greg: That's right.

Me: So I have to say, 'I really want this. I really am a thousand percent sure I want to win the lottery. $5 million, Lotto 6/49'. There's no doubt, it wouldn't ruin anything. (Laughing)

Greg: (Laughing hard)

Me: That's the only thing I am sure I want to do. The only thing I am really concerned about is my health. The only way to improve my condition is to get really healthy, working out.

Greg: Working out and balance.

Me: And rest, and relaxing. I don't see how that's possible working full-time right now, trying to do it all. I need to have more balance. Does Joe want to say anything else?

Greg: Yeah, he does. He wants you to know that he loves you more than anything. (Pause)
    Right now he's in front of your couch, he's down on one knee, as if he's proposing marriage, and he's is saying to you that he loves you more than anything. And he says you always have been and always will be his world... You're his world.... (Long pause)

Me: Was it supposed to be like this?

Greg: (Deep sigh) because he didn't voice what he should have voiced, yes, it was supposed to be this way.

Me: Because this was the course he was taking.

Greg: His whole life he didn't voice things! That was one of the things he was here to learn, and *you* were put here as a teacher for him to learn that.

Me: If he didn't make a mistake, would I have been able to help him?

Greg: Well, you were playing the role in terms of being able to help him.

Me: So I did what I could?

Greg: Right! He said you did what you could to help him. You know, you would ask him what was on his mind.

Me: I asked all the time. I don't think I even realized I was asking him so much. I am a very curious person.

Greg: You think? (Laughing at the sarcasm)

Me: I don't let things go, I always wonder why.

There were hard truths to face in this reading with Joe but I knew that Joe still loved me more than anything. He longed to hold me as much as I longed to hold him.

On the other side, Joe recognized that it was his responsibility to use his voice. This was one of his life's purposes in his incarnation, and he was unable to do this.

Things were put out there on the table as they were, but that did not make Joe's physical absence any easier. In hindsight, our souls have evolved in leaps and bounds since that reading in July of 2015. And now these issues in Joe's life seem small compared to what I was to soon uncover. What you will learn in the next chapter is the consequence of Joe's silent suffering from childhood abuse.

Chapter 10

A Fallen Rose's Thorns Remain

"They say love is eternal…They say love is enduring. It always protects, always hopes, always perseveres. Love never fails… It is one of my favourite passages from the bible…There is a quality about that kind of love that transcends our mortal understanding." ~ K.J. Kilton, Bella's Dilemma

My husband was the 3D (third dimensional) definition of success. He was handsome, sexy, athletic, intelligent, and friendly. He had a good paying job, a beautiful home and the family of his dreams. But still, he was a lost soul. His upbringing included struggles that left unhealed emotional wounds.

Joe did not seek the help and resources he needed and truly deserved. He was proud, and at the same time lived in such a defeated state that he was in denial that he was suffering from depression. How I wish Joe had sought help, seen our doctor and taken prescription medication.

However, something deep down inside of me felt that these may not have helped, at least not in the long run. Only months after Joe's death, I believed that Joe's wounds were so deep, so secret and so hidden that treatment may not have given him relief from the emotional pain that never ceased.

Joe was scarred by life. Unfortunately it was only after his death that I gained the clarity and understanding of what was happening with his mind, body and soul.

There were many factors that lead to Joe's downward spiral and ultimately his suicide. His mind, body and soul intricately wrapped around each other in a vortex of negativity, distress, and darkness. There were environmental factors; both negative and neutral but nothing positive was able to penetrate the toxic chemistry of his brain and cloudiness of his aura.

Joe was encapsulated in darkness, seemingly so that no light could get in. I wish I could have made the difference to turn his fate around. How I wish that Joe would have opened up to me and given me an opportunity to help him heal. I believe that love conquers all but we have to allow that love and that light in. That means setting our egos aside, not being proud and opening our hearts to the possibility that we can be healed. Prescription medication and psychotherapies may have helped and they may have saved his life in that moment of Joe's fatal mistake, until Joe's soul was ready to overcome and evolve from his past.

There had to be something positive to come out of such a tragedy. As difficult as it was, I was determined to bring something good out of my terrible loss. Like an invisible string that pulled me forward, I felt something deep in my soul that reminded me gently and firmly, *"Jen, you have to keep going, you have a job to do, God has you on an important mission. Keep going, in heaven you'll be proud of what you've done, and everything will seem like a bad dream then."*

I've heard often, that when we die we go through a Life Review. Our guides and Council of Elders gently show us our life like a movie or a hologram, and show us what we've done well and where we came up short. On the other side, we don't have an ego like on we do Earth, so when we see this, we are completely honest with ourselves, and never defensive or argumentative. We see other people's point of view and feelings.

It's comforting for me to think this happens in heaven. Since Joe's crossing over into the spiritual, I feel that I am more conscious and aware and try to review things from my higher self, to put my life choices into perspective.

This process of reviewing my life, especially at distressing times, has made me more aware of what is important in life. Our Creator in heaven is just and good, and will show everyone where they came up short and where there was room to do better. Those with integrity will breeze through their heavenly life reviews. Nobody is punished for their lives or their actions, so we never have to live in fear of dying.

Joe's death forced me to deal with the emotional issues and pain I faced from childhood to young adulthood. We married when I was only 23 so I never had a chance to deal with it on my own. Rather, I coped with my baggage in our marriage, just as Joe coped with his scars within our marriage. Joe and I grew up and matured together. We adored each other, and sensed in each other safety and respite with a tremendous sense of understanding. We also held the bar for one another. Both old souls with wisdom beyond our chronological years, we expected each other to pick ourselves up by the bootstraps and push ourselves to our external goals. Both of us were tough, but sometimes not the best listeners for each other. We held each other in shining gold light like a trophy proudly displayed on a shelf. Perhaps admittedly I did not want to see Joe's wounds. I wanted to make tangible improvements in our lives rather than dealing with Joe's emotional issues.

Deep inside we were connected. When we were together, our hearts were magnetically attracted to one another. There was passion, ecstasy and rapture. On the downside of this deep connection we felt each other's pain and so often the other's pain was easily felt as our own.

Joe and I lacked self-care. We became selfless martyrs only because we were forced to. Having a chronically ill child, a deceased child, and two young daughters and a family dog, without adequate support took its toll. We had the burden of care with our chronically ill son, but since Joe and I were both perfectionists, on the outside everything was rather well done, but nobody worked harder than us. We were a team in managing everything from laundry to dialysis.

The spiritual sense I was born with was unique to me rather than something that was instilled in us growing up. My parents had a lot of love for us and strong family values but I really didn't know what it meant to be loved and supported as an individual person. Like many, I was not taught self-love or that I had spiritual value.

Until my teen years I was a pretty happy, easy-going kid while we lived in my childhood home but I was really picked on as the youngest child. It may have been brotherly love but as a girl it was hard. I was the puppy at the bottom of the pile and it was easy for them to pick on someone smaller.

For the most part, I flew under the radar like I wanted to. I was quirky and had a good sense of humor as a kid. I had a few close friends and having so many older siblings did not make me overly precocious, but I had a spiritual awareness unlike other kids my age.

As I grew up tension in my home made me anxious to leave. I studied hard as I could to get into university and worked part-time at the local grocery store to afford the residence and tuition. By the time I graduated high school, I had saved over $10,000. I was accepted to university, but had little idea of what I wanted to do.

After Joe and I met in March of my last year of high school, I missed him terribly when we were apart, and in university I lived for the weekends to see him. At times, he was my only sanity in the world.

He was the nicest guy ever. He was the type of guy that moms love, and my mom did love him but perhaps worried about losing her youngest child once I met Joe. Unfortunately, Joe and I never had as much time together as I would have liked. His parents seemed to rely on him for many chores. He always had to be there for his parents, to be the man of the house and pick up for his father's lack. On top of that, he was usually working long hours, five or six days a week.

It wasn't until after Joe's death that I realized the scars that Joe carried from his childhood. To me, Joe was heroic with his family and always protective of the women in his life, but deep inside; there was a secret that Joe guarded with his life.

Sadly, just two months after Joe's death, I had a most unusual dream which triggered me to channel circumstances around Joe being sexually abused as a child. I dreamed of a haircut that Joe was getting in Montreal as a young boy returning from Europe. His mother and her sister were present. In the dream, Joe was getting his curly blonde locks cut into a short boy's haircut in the 1970s. The words that fell from his mother's mouth were so shocking that it woke me from a sound sleep. Joe's Mother was telling Joe's Aunt about the sexual abuse he suffered in Europe, and I woke up to the words, "He was molested" coming from his mother's voice.

In the middle of that sound sleep, I woke up in shock knowing that this dream was meant to reveal something to me that had been deliberately kept secret from me during my entire relationship with Joe. That night, I began to look back as I laid still in my bed, pondering if there was truth in my dream. For the hours and days that followed, I began to channel from

Joe the circumstances around his alleged abuse. I was still raw with grief and just beginning to process the tremendous loss I was experiencing. I was deeply depressed, and the stressors and conflict with my family were mounting. I was at the bottom of a very deep well and all the ties to lift me out were like ropes fraying from the tension, about to break at any moment. I could barely hold on and I feared how fragile I was. I felt that anymore weight would sever the cords and I would fall eternally into a deep dark pit of eternal hell and suffering.

That could well be an understatement because there are no words to describe the pain I felt. I did everything I could to be well, desperate to be there for my children. The disapproval and pressure of my family were burdens I had to bare on top of the losses I suffered.

I'm not sure why this information was given to me just a little more than two months after Joe's death. But it gave me greater compassion for the husband whose death I felt victimized by. I saw him as a vulnerable little child, rather than a tough man who had turned his family into victims of his death. Perhaps it also provided some explanation of his pain, and shame of asking for help. However, this was coupled by the disbelief that he hid the information from me for so many years as if I was not a trustworthy partner, capable of understanding and providing sufficient nurturing. I do know in retrospect, that this information probably gave me a welcome distraction to my own pain. Perhaps, it helped me focus on Joe, leading me to have some compassion and reasoning for his death.

Over the next days, while still in shock, I began to channel Joe and connect the dots from the past to the abuse. I began to have flashbacks to times when I felt very unsatisfied by explanations and comments, yet when I had pressed deeper and with more intent, my inquiries were brushed off, leaving me feeling unsettled, but never consciously believing there was so much more to the story that the tiny tip of the iceberg I could just barely sense was there. The way I was dismissed left me feeling as if I was only imagining the tip of an iceberg at all.

I remember things that had been done and said over the past few years to sweep everything connected to these incidents under the rug. I was dumbfounded. All the conversations about this particular relative in Europe had been shut down and it left me asking many questions. However, these were only subtle clues that left me scratching my subconscious mind, and I never would have guessed that something was deliberately being hidden from me.

I remembered things from sixteen years before Joe's death when Joe was grieving our son Joseph to just a few days before Joe's death. All those question marks I could not let go of had clear explanations behind them. The truth was being hidden from me. The illusion that was created for me to protect me, ultimately created a weapon that formed against me by taking what was most precious to me, because if I had known, maybe I could have saved my beloved from the psychological trauma he endured.

Months after our son Joseph's death, which was in January of 1999, Joe and I had a Mother's Day dinner to attend at my family's house. I remember, Joe was depressed and secluded himself in his basement workshop of our home. I tried my best to cheer him up and make him feel better. Eventually with coercion we finally left for my sister's, but when my frustration with him got the better of me, he jumped out of our vehicle only to walk home. He refused to come back and I ended up going with young Nicholas alone.

We were there for just a short time, when my brother began to bug me about what I had done to cause Joe not to join us. I immediately began to get upset because I was so hurt by Joe's behaviour. Things began unravelling when my sister tried to take control of the situation by bringing up her problems with Joe. She didn't understand that Joe and I were still grieving the death of our son only months before and she especially did not understand the magnitude of the emotions Joe was facing. Things escalated quickly and I started to feel that everybody was ganging up on me. I felt both compassion and betrayal for my partner Joe, even though I could not understand his side of things because I did not know the truth of what was really going on in his mind. As I was leaving I remember saying the strangest words, "Everybody knows his dirty little secret" and wondered why I had used that term. It felt like a gross exaggeration of what I was going through. My Dad's sturdy words provided sanity to my spinning head. He told me that everybody needs to have a good long hard look at themselves, and he was going to have a word with Joe.

When I got home, I told Joe how he ruined my Mother's Day and he apologized as I cried, seeing the pain he had caused. I never got an explanation as to what was bothering him that day. But in hindsight I

Jennifer Angelee

recognize that he was not only dealing with grief over losing Joseph, or his own depression, he was beginning to remember the sexual abuse he had suppressed over twenty years before. He was beginning to blame himself, believing that he was being punished by losing his second born son, his namesake, Joseph.

I began to remember more recent events the days after the dream that seemed to lead to the circumstances around the alleged sexual abuse. The details of these memories are so evidential that I at last understood all of the weird comments and attitudes that puzzled me. For example, about six months before Joe died, a relative made a comment about another relative regarding Joe's difficulties learning to read. This relative was supposed to be teaching him to read but I was told that something else was going on by someone close to the situation. I briefly questioned Joe in the car on the ride home and I let it go without an answer. Joe had quickly dismissed my question and became distant.

Joe had a relative that died of cancer in Europe in 2012, the same summer that our son had his transplant. That same relative had attempted to contact me on more than one occasion after his own death. In fact, the night of his death, I was awoken in the middle of the night to a loud ring that sounded like a flat line on a heart monitor. It was very scary because I was alone in the house and I had no idea what it was. The next day I learned unexpectedly of his death from cancer, though I was completely unaware he had been sick. Given the nature of the family, I thought his untimely death had passed with little significance. I thought they were a close and sentimental family and I assumed he would have a special memorial mass but did not.

The last trip we took as a family was the March Break before Joe's death in May. We drove to Florida from Ontario. We weren't on the road an hour in the early hours of the morning when Joe became sullen and withdrawn. Bored and trying to liven things up, I said to Joe, "Let's talk. It's a long drive; let's talk to pass the time." Joe was uptight and said he didn't feel like talking, and after we crossed the border and we were in New York State, I began to have terrible chest pain. A little worried, I reviewed my medical history with Joe, but he seemed totally unconcerned, even angry with me. I didn't understand why I was suffering because I was happy to be getting away with the kids and we had anticipated this trip with joy for months.

Things only became tenser and by evening we were still driving, and I asked Joe insistently that he tell me what was wrong. He told me "A lot of things."

"Like what?" I said.

He replied. "Like my childhood and my learning disability."

I told him that lots of people have learning disabilities and so does our son; that he needs to be a role model, and besides how much did any of that matter since he was successful in all ways and had a good job?

Joe replied as I pressed harder for the truth. It didn't make sense to me what he was keeping to himself. I asked him what the 'big secret' is. He told me he couldn't tell me because he was protecting me and the kids.

"From what??" I retorted, "Are you having an affair? I know that's not it, you wouldn't do that, would you? Why won't you tell me?"

Joe insisted I drop it as I became more aggravated. The tension between us was mounting, and eventually we stopped at a motel for the night. The next day we continued to Florida. The kids and I were excited to cross the border, but Joe was angry for no apparent reason. By evening we checked into our condo on the beach and it wasn't until that night with much insistence that Joe and I began to communicate.

Joe was very sad. We had a good heart to heart talk, and he told me that he felt I didn't want him around. I told him that was ridiculous, and just because I'm busy and distracted, it didn't mean I was losing interest in him. He seemed receptive and we went to bed together.

Joe continued to be withdrawn for the trip. The first day on the beach, Joe went up to the room to get some drinks and snacks for us and took an awfully long time. I was irritated when he returned, and I didn't care to notice that he had been crying when gone, but looking back I remember the look in his eyes and the expression on his face.

Our last evening in Florida, our kids were content after a long day, and stayed in the room to watch TV. Joe and I went for our last walk on the beach at sunset. The sunset was remarkable. I told Joe, "See, this is what I want to do with you every night when we retire." Joe didn't reply. I have a picture of the back of him facing the beautiful sunset over the ocean. Something about that photograph tells a sad story that Joe knew that was

Jennifer Angelee

his last sunset and the reason he didn't respond to me is because he felt he would not be with me for those sunset walks.

That holiday was the first time I consciously became aware that Joe had clinical depression. I was carefully monitoring his state as I could afford the time as we went about our busy lives. I was fully prepared to tell Joe when it was time to see our doctor but I never expected he was suicidal. Because Joe was so full of repressed anger, I often felt blamed and felt guilty around him. Instead of blaming his moods on him, I blamed myself. He was so frustrating, pushing my buttons until I'd slip and say something out of frustration, then he would be very cunning in turning his anger toward me. Eventually I began to wear his depression like a curse, causing me to buckle like a broken doll. Joe never gave me the satisfaction of winning anything. My knee began to collapse when I walked. My medical problems surmounted. My doctor even suggested a hysterectomy. My body was unravelling as I carried the unspoken burden of pain of my husband. Something was very wrong and it wasn't until my reading with Carol Righton on August 7, 2015, that I confirmed my suspicions about my husband's tainted past.

Reading with Carol Righton - August 7, 2016

"I have died everyday waiting for you. Darling, don't be afraid. I have loved you for a thousand years. I'll love you for a thousand more." -Christina Perri

As Carol used the Tibetan singing bowl to clear the space to call in my soul guides and higher self, she reported a presence of the angelic realm. Mother Teresa, Mother Mary and Divine Mother were called in with the Archangels. The Divine Mother and Mother Teresa were called in to release the pain. Mother Mary's mother, Anne was called in to help hold my loss and my heart. I breathed in deeply and began to cry. I breathed in the wisdom of the Divine Mother, and surrendered to Mother Mary in my suffering, who said, "For a minute, let me carry your pain." Carol said these women were 'pulling the pain body off of me, pulling the energy of pain that is covering me off of me.'

Mother Teresa said she is pulling the pain body off into Christ

Consciousness. She said it isn't serving me anymore. She said she is pulling it off so that I can move into the source of peace. Mother Teresa said, "We don't expect you to get over it quickly, but we want to offer you peaceful moments."

I felt Mother Mary holding me in her vibration of peace. I could feel the light around my shoulders. Carol reported that Mother Mary was holding me and patting my head saying, "There is no shame, honey, there is no shame. Don't be in shame; don't be in guilt for one moment. I will hold it for you. I will hold it for you for this moment."

Archangel Chamuel's light came around me, as I breathed in and out deeply while crying. A huge release was taking place and for those moments I felt the comfort and peace of the divine feminine energies with me, as they held me and told me to breathe like a small baby.

They said there are two times when I should let them hold the pain for me. One time is first thing in the morning, light a candle and call in Mother Mary, Saint Teresa and Mother Teresa, who were with me. The other time is before I go to bed.

"In those moments just surrender and give us permission to hold it for you." Crying I replied, "First thing in the morning is the hardest."

They also said for me to take a hot bath in the morning, and I may have to get up a bit early. They said, "Sea salt, light a candle, just let us hold it for you."

I told Carol, "I've been trying to get up and go in the pool." She asked me if the pool was salt water, which it is. The divine women were telling me to get up and go in my pool. Carol said light white candles, call them in and say, "Mother Mary, Teresa, Divine Mother, come and hold my pain body."

Carol said that the aspect of God which is the Divine feminine was not written in the Bible, in scripture, but the divine feminine Mother is wisdom, nurturing, and intelligent, like the moon energy. She said "You have a very strong connection to the divine father energy, the sun, which is intense, and demanding. They are asking you to get more in touch with the divine feminine energy. Actually I feel you are going to write more through divine mother, she will help you."

Through my tears I asked, "Can I ask you my questions?"

"Yes, sure."

"Why did this terrible thing have to happen, especially to me?"

"The sad thing about is this is not all about you. You are the consequence. It is not happening to you. You are the consequences of it. Was it supposed to happen? No! Was it divinely written? That's what they call accidents. These are the consequences, shifts of things not in plan. These are the things of Earth that are not predictable. They are saying that you are the consequence of the energies action. Did you write this in your plan? No, so stop taking responsibility for it, you did not write it in your plan."

"Divine Mother says, 'Like the planet, what we hear, think, know and feel can be produced. This was not your energy; it was the energy of your husband. They say that you were not responsible or to be accountable for it. This was not written in this lifetime for you. She says the consequences of being in a human body in life are very difficult and very depressing and sad. She is showing me that this is the circumstances of the vibration of humanity coming through his soul. Do you understand that?"

"My husband's soul?"

"Yeah, he is saying you are not responsible. You are not responsible for his choices. Each one of us is responsible for our own actions. He made his own choices. He is showing me, it was his choice to surrender into the light."

"But it was kind of an accident for him. Once he did it, he realized he made a mistake. I don't understand. (Crying) Why did he do this to me?"

"He said, you know the sad thing is you're the consequences of his action. He didn't do it to you. His thought was relieving of stress and pain of self, stress and pain of self."

"But could I have done something to make that pain go away? Did I cause the pain?"

"No. He says the pain has always been there since he was about five or six years old. Did he talk to you about that? His pain was always there. It started when he was a young child. He said he 'possessed and held pain'. It's an interesting term. When he was young, hmm, you know what he just said? 'I came in sad; my first breath was of sadness.' His journey was to get through the sadness without someone showing him how – about conquering sadness of self. He was always made to feel like there was something wrong with him as a child. Did you know that?"

"Yeah, I know."

"Okay, good, because he's saying they always made me feel like there was something wrong with me, as if he just took on and possessed that vibration. So he said if everyone is saying there is something wrong, there must be something wrong."

Quickly and quietly I said, "Was he abused?"

"How much has he talked to you about that?"

"In hindsight, not a lot of details."

"Um, I get the feeling he was sexually abused."

"That is what I was going to ask you… he was molested?"

"Yes, I got the word right away."

"I had a dream the other night…"

I quickly explained the dream to her, and asked the specific questions I needed for confirmation of my suspicions. I decided not to include the details in my final edit of this book.

"Uh, I didn't figure this abuse out until last week."

"It's interesting because he didn't have a lot of recall of it. After the death of your son, he remembered the shame."

"That is why he was so depressed, in a different way," I said.

"Um-hmm. He remembered the shame. He felt like,…like he was being punished."

"Like when Joseph died, he felt that was a punishment?"

Carol replied to me, "And it is interesting because he, this is so sad, as a child he blamed himself because 'I'm calling it in', especially around the age of seven. At three he didn't realize, at age seven he said, 'I must be doing something wrong here, because this keeps happening to me'. He never spoke up about it, so he felt shame for not speaking up."

I replied, "He wouldn't tell me this."

"It's sad because the adult self of him felt so responsible for what happened to him. It was all about shame. He said that I am responsible." (Crying hard) "I wish he told me, I could have helped him."

He said, "I made that choice though, not to share. I am responsible for not telling you. It was not up to you to guess."

"He didn't remember it until the tragedy of your son, and then it came back so fast, he didn't know how to handle it…he remembered everything (deep breath). There were some harsh disciplines that he received when he was younger, so he was taught not to speak. Keep the family shame, keep the family quiet, don't speak, don't tell."

Carol and I continued our conversation in detail about the male energies of the past in spirit. She once again confirmed my suspicions of specific details, "Yes, there is something with that. They are moving forward, (softly whispering) 'Shhh, it's not talked about, shhh'."

I added, "Months before I got a hint because something that was happening seemed so senseless. I never got a reason why it was happening. But this is the only thing that makes sense."

"There is something very secretive there, so when they are ready to share, it will come forth."

"What do you mean they are ready to share? Like, no one alive is going to say anything!?!"

Carol replied to me, "No I mean the other side. It's interesting the vibration is saying, it's not ready yet. It's not time yet."

"Is this what caused him to do what he did?'

"I am getting, yes."

"Huh" (deep sigh)

"You're not the cause."

"No, but it bothers me that this is the cause, and now my kids don't have a father. (Crying). Why couldn't he talk to me about it?"

"The thing is you're asking him to talk about something that was so suppressed in his family, you were asking him to talk about something that he was so traumatized by, he was barely coming to terms with it. Do you understand that?"

"He's saying, 'There is such shame in my family, there is such shame.'" (Crying) "Is my life ever going to be okay? I just feel like he is the only man I have ever loved, or could ever love. I was still in love with him, and I would have done anything for him."

"He knows that too. He just wished he could…he was just so overwhelmed. He says, 'I just got so overwhelmed, so overwhelmed…'"

"And I am being punished for what he did."

"Why, who's blaming you?"

"Someone close said that this would not have happened if I was not the way I am."

"You are not responsible for someone else taking their life."

"I think his parents blame me."

"Well of course, they don't want to face the facts, of coming to the realization of reality. Something happened to him when he was a child, that age when he was 5 and 7 is very prominent, and he says his family is in such denial, that if you faced it with them, they would deny it."

"Was he the only one?"

"He keeps saying this is the family secret. Joe says you are right on with your thinking. Keep following your truth. He says you must not allow them to make you feel responsible for this. He said you know in your deepest heart, you are not responsible for this. He says, 'I'm responsible because I should have come into the truth'."

"I know that you're feeling the consequences, but in his next life, he will feel the consequences as well."

"What do you mean?"

"He didn't have the confidence in himself to share this. He thought, if I share this, she'll leave me… (As I shake my head) you don't understand how a person has been wounded, when you're in pain, your mind is not rationale."

(Crying) "Oh I know that."

"Can I ask you how he passed?" Carol asked.

"He hung himself."

"Okay because he keeps showing me his wrists together, he says his hands were bound."

"I don't think he did that."

"He's referring to his childhood, his hands were bound."

"It's weird though, intimately we had the best relationship. It was completely normal."

"After your son passed, there was an opening, and he was in denial of it, he didn't get help. He didn't recognize, he didn't know, feel, and understand."

I explained, "When I began to heal in the spring after my son died, he began to close himself off. It was very devastating to him".

"He didn't share because he didn't know how to, he couldn't get a handle on it. The energy just came in and slammed him."

"One of the things we have to work through with you is releasing shame and guilt. There is time that goes with that, what Mother Teresa and Mother Mary are saying is, once in the morning and once at night, please let us hold this for you."

"Will I ever be happy again? Is it even possible?"

"You will always feel his loss. You will feel happy, but there will always be part of you that will honour that aspect of yourself. There will always be an energy that always honours that relationship. You are not meant to forget that relationship, and all the beautiful things in the relationship. Right now, Mother Mary says it makes you feel sad, but you will move into a phase of honouring the relationship. He really wants to make clear that you are not responsible; I don't know why anyone is thinking that you're responsible. If he knew the consequences that this was going to cause; you couldn't stop it. It was a thought that came in so fast; this guy wasn't planning to do this. One moment he said, that's it."

"The day he died was the only day I gave up on him and decided not to talk to him. He was making me depressed and I went back to bed. That was the only day of my life that I've given up and done that to him. But I wasn't doing it to him. I just did nothing because everything I tried with him failed."

Carol continued, "It's really sad that everybody is making you feel responsible. He said it was *my* choice. He says that he sees that you were abused emotionally. He says to tell you to 'Please keep going. Look in the faces of your children'. He says, 'It's not pretty'. He says we have to repeat our lives over in the same pain we left in. Yes we are over here healing, but one of our causes and affect is that we have to come into this planet and relive the pain to get through this'. He says, 'It's not a picnic, you definitely get reincarnated', and this is coming from your son, 'You definitely get incarnated again, you definitely get put back on this planet, and you definitely come back with the emotions that you leave on'. He says that is part of divine."

"Will we have another life together? He said third time is a charm… When I die, will he be waiting for me?"

"He said the choice will be yours. They are honouring you because they want you to have the best life here that you possibly can."

"Who is *they*?"

"The divine energy, the angelic energy, they are saying, 'We're honouring her, this is her decision'. Actually, there will be a meeting on the other side. There will be communication, giving him the strength to come back here, and make it through."

"Will he make it up to me in the next life without causing anymore pain?"

"It's interesting because he says, 'Everyone experiences everything in life. At one point in time, everyone experiences suicide. You have already experienced it, so you do not have to experience it again. He says for everyone who experiences suicide, life gets tougher."

"I want to say this; this is coming from the angelic realm: Everyone experiences suicide, everyone experiences murder, everyone pain, everyone experiences war, hunger, and everyone experiences luxury, and so what he is showing me is that everyone experiences every vibration. He says that suicide vibrations are interesting because you only get one shot at that. He says you've already experienced it once, after that it gets much harder, more challenging. He says you've already experienced it once, please keep going."

"So, I've already died by suicide?"

"He says we all have. If you want it to be 'third time is a charm, than you mustn't do that in this lifetime'. He says you must push through." (Crying) "But what are the good things I have to live for because I only feel like half a person? I'm missing him. There is a huge void."

"Did you know that he held space when you did it in a past lifetime?"

"What do you mean he held space?"

"When you did it he held space for you on this planet."

"What do you mean? He was with me?"

"Yes, he was there and held space when you took your own life."

"Each one of us experiences everything in life. That is why there is no judgement. We experience all aspects of ourselves, of humanity. So the reason he is saying third time is a charm, is you went through your evolutional experience, he held the light, took care of the family, took care of things, now you are."

"Oh because I thought in one lifetime that he went to war and I died in childbirth and he allowed himself to be killed. I went for a past life reading last year and I was told that."

"Yes, but what he is talking about with 'third time is a charm' is the synchronicity of the suicides, first you, then him, and third time is a charm. This was his soul's turn to experience it. Ying and yang, we must experience doing it and having it done. The soul wants to come to this planet so it can experience all aspects of emotion in a body, in the physical. It is familiar with spiritual and energetic because that is what divine is. Life is about feeling emotions, we want to feel what it is like to experience emotions in a body. How does it feel? So you went first, that was your experience, and for every side both will feel it, both will experience it. You're like soul mates, or like soul partners, very much part-*ners* in the evolution of your soul. So when you said, 'Will I go back to him?' Yeah you will, he's going to wait, he knows his debt. He's saying please don't do that to yourself because if you do that to yourself, you're not going to meet, because you will meet in a lower vibration."

"So what do I have to look forward to in this life? I have everything I want, except him. No money is going to make a difference; I think I will just use the money to cross all the things off the bucket list for the kids…"

"He's saying to you, 'Your journeys are to re-connect and get through it. He's saying 'You're going to get through it'. This is both of your souls learning. That is why there will always be an aspect of your soul honouring him. There will always be a part of yourself that feels like you lost your left arm, but you will move into an acceptance with that, and understand that you're going to feel the loss, but if you keep going, raising the children, fulfilling your contract, the two of you can reunite and create a new one. Keep your focus, please, please."

"I just have a feeling it's going to be a very long time in this body. I just have a feeling it's going to be a long life. So what am I going to do?"

"See your daughter's wedding, see your son or daughter's graduations. I want you to see your children when they have their children. Take your kids and explore the planet, travel. Every time you lose faith, see your children's futures, your daughter's babies. Move into bringing forth moments for your children. Don't look at how you can ever love again, because that is what is breaking your heart, you're looking down the wrong path. Look down the path of the future of all the beautiful moments you would miss with your children. He says take the children away at Christmas to somewhere warm, swim with dolphins on Christmas morning, let them have some experiences. Show them the beauty of the world. Heal through the beauty of the planet. You must continue, it's very important to your contract."

"He says travel with your kids, your going to be very inspired."

"I am nervous."

"Travel to Ireland, England, Hawaii is beautiful…What you're going to find is your book is going into cause and effect. Your love story is not finished yet. Your love story is not over."

Reflecting back on this reading over a year after it took place, it was as if a light bulb went off. At the time of the reading I was in so much pain and in so much shock, I did not intellectually comprehend the larger lessons and messages as deep and profound. I was in the depths of despair, almost hell bound, on the edge of surviving my torment. Looking back I am in awe at the depth of human, physical emotion I experienced, and the idea that such powerful spiritual energies can step in so personally to hold pain for us.

The lessons for me are profound. Admittedly, I neglected to take advantage of the healing power of these feminine energies to hold my pain. In my pain, I simply forgot. In hindsight, I wish I had remembered and been more open as I am now. On the other hand, looking back, I have changed.

Now, I look back on what I was feeling and experiencing in those moments and I have compassion for myself. I forgive myself for not being perfect at that time, and I am of course relieved that I made it through those most tortuous months. My husband's messages were accurate and I learned to listen to the small voice of hope inside of me. Failure was not an option. I had to be here for my children. My soul had to survive and overcome my loss. I had to not only find the light, I had to become the light for myself and my children. I became the brave warrior soul I was destined to be as an eternal being, and my life became more purposeful.

As Carol said, I have come to a greater acceptance of not only honouring myself and my emotions but of honouring Joe. It took a long time for me to get to a place of honour, and though I still struggle with acceptance, I have come a long way.

The healing power of these readings has given me great causal explanations. I have almost fully come to dissolving guilt and self-blame, and within these messages, Joe always takes full responsibility for ending his own life. The more I come to accept that his suicide was his choice of surrender, the more I am able to accept his death and live my own life.

It wasn't until writing this and hearing the recording again that I realized the profound universal messages about suicide. When I went for these readings, I did not see how they would be used in my book. In fact, I was not driven to have these readings for the purposes of sharing them in a book. I was driven my innate desire to know the truth. I was in a ball of confusion when my life was turned upside down and my soul was shook so bad, I was between what I would call 'as close to hell as you can get' and my life which was a living nightmare.

The way we are taught to perceive death in society inevitably leaves the bereaved to feel hopeless and can obscure their perception of living life without their deceased loved one. But the pain of grief can be made more bearable if we realize that feeling despair is a 'normal' feeling that we can move through. Feeling hopeless is a normal feeling when someone especially close to us dies. Unfortunately, our despair can make those in society feel uncomfortable, and the bereaved are sometimes told insensitive things and expected to snap out of grief quickly.

What this can do to the mind of the bereaved is it can make them feel more alone and isolated. It can create a tunnel vision into a depression where hopeful options seem invisible.

We need people who can help the bereaved see the hope in their lives. Where they can move forward and co-create in the physical even with their loved one in spirit. The spirits of our deceased loved ones live on and can advocate for the preciousness and value of life for those they leave behind. They want the best for us. They want us to feel joy and live our lives to the fullest.

Carol's explanation of karma is remarkable. When another clairvoyant friend reported that I had died by suicide in a past life, and it was karma that was being balanced, and the debt was paid, I felt I was being punished in this life for a past life mistake. "What kind of God or Universe is this that we live tortured in a karmic cycle where everything is tit for tat?" I was a little annoyed by this causal explanation for Joe's death by suicide. After all, our children should not suffer for our mistakes, we weren't just talking about Joe and I as partners and soul mates, but innocent children who now have to grow up without their beloved father.

After this reading, I stepped into my new role as single mother more assuredly. I refused to allow my children to fall victim and be more disadvantaged than they had to be. Never being one to do anything half-hearted, I ascended into my new role with clarity and precision. I declared to my children that our home is a place of love where fear has no place, and that everything we did, we did out of love. Acknowledging the destructive affects of fear in the greatest magnitude possible (someone taking their own life) gave me an awareness few others could possess. Each time I felt the detrimental affects that the downward spiral of fear precipitates, I thought of the love I wanted to share with my children. I began to look to the future with bigger plans in my head.

Learning to trust God took on a whole new meaning. I had to trust a Universe that betrayed me, that allowed a colossal accident to happen. In doing so I became a conscious co-creator of my destiny. But I did not know exactly what my destiny was. I still don't. What I do know is that the old way of living couldn't work anymore. In my heart, I had to be the best version of me possible, and I have a lot to do before I meet Joe in Heaven. I know he is proud of me, and I know he is guiding me. I think I'm even teaching him from the other side. I think he is saying, "Jeez, I never thought of that. You're so smart – you're amazing!"

Lastly, I think there is a huge Universal message being brought forth here about judgement and forgiveness. As was said, we all have been murderers, all died by suicide, all of us have been thieves, lived in luxury, and so on. We have experienced every emotion in the physical body so that we may know ourselves greater. This makes me think back to scripture where Jesus says, "Whoever is without sin may cast the first stone." This is a powerful statement about judgement and about forgiveness.

The world that Joe left me in was so cold that it made me realize that I was truly the only suitable and loving guardian for my children. I had seen how fearful many people in our world had become. I agonized over who would be my children's guardian if I died. I learned to trust God that I will be there to support my beloved kids and to trust God with my future.

Chapter 11

Forgiveness is the Fragrance of the Rose

"When one forgives, two souls are set free." ~ Unknown

As September approached, I knew I needed to go back to work, to be with people in a familiar environment. I was anxious about working without the support of my husband in our home but my fear made my determination stronger.

As broken as I was, I needed to know that I was capable of being a single working mother. I had lost Joe's substantial income and I didn't know if there would be enough to support us and maintain the house on one income. When I returned to work, I was still in shock, still grief struck. I had a large lawn to mow and that September I bought myself a battery operated lawn mower and sold my corded electrical mower on Kijiji. Small victories like this made me realize that I was becoming stronger, wiser and more self-sufficient in life.

The kids and I pulled together to make it work. Nicholas was returning for his last year of high school to upgrade in order to apply to a university degree program in computer science. Faith entered grade seven and Hope grade four. Somehow, the kids learned quickly to help with meals, and do the dishes, but it was often tough to coax my youngest and oldest to do their fair share. Nicholas became my little handy man, and helped with technical things like the floor cleaner for our inground pool. That thing must weigh 100 pounds and I could not pull it out of the water. Somehow this young man of only a bit over 100 pounds himself, had resources of strength to get done what needed to be done.

Beloved, I Can Show You Heaven

When I returned to work the September following Joe's death, I wasn't ready in many ways, but I also wasn't ready to stay home with the pain in my heart. I needed a change, any change. It hurt to be home alone without the man who filled our house with his infectious energy and made our house a home. The worst thing about my work day used to be my favourite. I used to walk to my vehicle in anticipation of seeing my beloved husband when I got home. Often he marched out the door to my van to help me with my belongings and to greet me with a kiss and a hug, welcoming me home. Coming home without him became the worst part of my day. It was absolutely dreadful. I remember the first sombre weekend of the school year. What a dreadful Friday it was. I missed the time that Joe and I spent together. Friday had been our day of re-uniting since the early days of university. He was always freshly showered when I got home from work, smelling like the roses he had always given me so many years before. I would breathe him in and with each embrace, life seemed only to exist within the heart shaped aura that would enclose the both of us like the touch of God.

I clearly remember the funk I was in and what I did to get myself out of it. It was after school the Friday of that first weekend back to school. I was extra attentive to my kids and read with my angel cards in the pretty front living room of our home. I gave Faith an angel card reading and I thought it went really well. I remember the angels telling her to focus on her art, but more so I recall the incredible feeling that lifted me out of my grief for a brief time. I felt that in giving the reading from a higher level, I was fulfilling a purpose that I wanted to use to help others. This inspired me to investigate Angel Guidance and Healing at my next opportunity.

I was still numb and in shock from Joe's death and I didn't really know it. The next Monday evening I went to see a Spiritual Psychotherapist, named Nadia. She is also an Angel Guidance Practitioner and this was the first time I spoke to someone about the guilt and blame I was holding in the four months since Joe's death. From every convoluted thing I had been told by my family and the non-communication from Joe's parents, in some way I truly believed that Joe's death was my fault. I had been keeping all the circumstances around Joe's death to myself out of shame. I felt my negligence had caused his death and if only I had done so many things differently, then Joe would still be alive. Part of me believed that the pain I was feeling was the punishment and consequences of my personality or behaviour.

Through the release of many, many tears, I finally let go and cried. Until then, it was not safe to cry. As I told Nadia all the details, she asked me how I felt afterward. I was so relieved when she told me I was not to blame for Joe's suicide, and she seemed so unsurprised as she held space for me as my emotion poured out. This seemed like the normal events of a suicide death to her, I was not the exception.

But it took more than this one time to put my guilt and shame to rest and peace. Though I had taken the first step, the hardest one, I was on my way with the support of the universe to help me with this crucial step to healing. My mind felt the need to check in and revisit the logic that blamed myself. Perhaps my guilt was easier to bear than the anger I could not face with Joe. It was too overwhelming for me to be angry with someone who had become a ghost of his former self. My anger was palpable and as real as the nose on my face. I wanted to punch Joe with all my might for causing the unnecessary suffering he had caused us. He had ruined every aspect of life. I was too angry to forgive him, too angry to honour him, but eventually my lack of forgiveness began to hurt me both energetically and physically. Nothing was fair anymore, nothing. Each job I did that used to be Joe's made me bitter with emotions that overwhelmed me. On top of that I was dealing with three children who were broken-hearted and fragile.

When cleaning off papers from my desk at home, I had come across the number of a woman I had befriended sixteen months earlier in an angel communication workshop. Her name was Sandra. Sandra was a Medium and we seemed to hit it off like school girls in the workshop, always chatting and having much to say. We exchanged numbers since we had made a connection with each other. One day after work, I decided out of loneliness to call Sandra and see what she was up to. She returned my call later that evening and I asked her lots of questions of what she had been up to. I did not tell her what had been happening with me at all.

I decided to book a reading with her and see where it led. I felt from where I was I had nothing to lose.

On September 26th, I had a phone reading with Sandra that evening from home. The first thing she talked about was *Forgiveness*. She told me I needed to release something a person did to me. She said there is a male energy around me that passed more recently and that I was really taken by this, that I loved this person a lot and that I did a lot for this person. She expressed how important it is to my heart to forgive this person. She did not know my husband had died, and was shocked and very sorry when I told her.

After learning this, the reading continued the following evening. Sandra had meditated on the mediumship reading that afternoon. She told me that Joe is still in the process of his life review and he is very loving.

On the phone I sat earnestly at my kitchen table listening:

Sandra: He's very much around in the home and he loves everybody. He's full of joy. (*He tried to tell her how he passed. She respectfully told him she was not ready for that*).

Your grandmother is with you. I got the feeling that she is somebody's spirit guide. She talked about the teddy bear that she gave you when you were a little girl, about four or five years old. The thing I love about this is it shows me who you are: I was taken to a section that felt very angelic and loving where you used to see angels yourself, you're very much connected to angels. I saw that your son is very much connected to angels as well. This comes from your mother's side by the way.

Me: It does, I was just thinking of that this morning.

Sandra: Nicholas is also very spiritually intelligent. As crazy as it sounds, he was chosen to be the first witness to his father's passing. Your grandmother expressed love to him for the way that he handled his father's death.

Me: I don't know how he found the fortitude to do what he did. Everybody blamed me that Nicholas was the one to find him. It was Nicholas' sixth sense and his insistence to come home. He knew instinctively what Joe had done. I was in a daze. It was a bit of a role reversal.

Sandra: I felt his courage and bravery. He was chosen for this role. What other 17 year old could accomplish something like that and not pass out?

Me: Incredibly he is smaller than me. He's only 110 pounds.

Sandra: I am so proud of him. He was meant to do this; it was part of his contract. One day Jen, it's going to make sense to you. You just have let go of the guilt and emotional attachment to what other people think.

Me: I've talked to at least three people this week about my guilt. People I tell at work are surprised I feel guilty.

Sandra: Especially since you're an empath. If you can just release that last little bit of guilt, I see you being a spiritual healer. Like people coming into your home or you're working in the community, doing this and healing others. You are truly a healer/empath/intuitive. You have such beautiful blue light around you. I was in such awe. I rarely see that, it's very beautiful, very angelic. The only thing is I feel the distance, I feel the gap.

Me: I feel the distance with him too and I was closer to him than anybody. Why is he distant? He was very much around at the beginning. Is it because of his own regret around the way he left? He was never one to impose on me. He was always very considerate. I think he's afraid of hurting me.

Sandra: Well, I've heard that suicides don't really want to leave; they remain very much around the home.

Me: I know he wasn't thinking, and that's an understatement. It was like a heart attack of the brain. He was very messed up.

Sandra: You know all this happened because there was past life karma. You did something similar in a past life. The karma is totally cleared, I felt the energy, and I asked my guides and angels. He said that, 'When my wife is ready, I would like to talk with my wife.' You are going to meet in the next life together. He is going to come and get you when it is your time to leave the planet. He kept insisting, 'I am willing to meet with my wife whenever she wants to contact me'. He was very gentle with me but there was that distance. It was like when you cannot pick up a radio station right but there is that sound? Grandma was there the whole time; she's very strong in spirit, highly evolved. She said she was the one who gave you the teddy bear; she loves you, not to worry and continue with your psychic ability.

Me: When Hope was a little girl, she was very psychic. It was amazing; she talked about her Grandma all the time. She was a very powerful kid, a bit of a strong-willed trouble maker like my husband. It makes sense that if Joe is often with her, that my grandmother is there as well.

Beloved, I Can Show You Heaven

Sandra: Your Grandmother is quite funny actually because every time she barges in. She kept coming in, like if I was having a conversation with your husband, she just came in and spoke, and she knows what she's talking about. She's very highly evolved. She is so highly evolved that she is a spirit guide.

Me: When Hope was little, I saw my grandmother when I closed my eyes, not in my mind, but under my lids. Does that make sense Sandra?

Sandra: Oh yes!

Me: She had a classic style. Her brown dress with white polka dots was now crisp and black with white polka dots, a little more dressed up. She was walking on the street. It reminded me of a classic Disney scene.

Sandra: Joe is very much in the home and around your daughter Hope. Your grandmother and him are saying they have met and they are together.

Me: I met Joe five months after my Grandma died. I always told him that she would have really liked him, to her he would have been the perfect man, the way he was so handy and hard-working.

Sandra: He's very calm, loving, and compassionate. I was surprised I was dealing with a suicide, but my higher self said that this was his souls plan. Your grandmother is very involved. She came in and out four or five times. She also put her hand on my left shoulder and said, "Just tell her she is going to be okay."

Me: That makes me feel good, that someone in the family is watching us.

Sandra: Well, your husband is too.

Me: But I have not accepted his death. I don't know how much of a helper he is in spirit; like he was in body.

Sandra: It's beautiful the way he is holding you, such divine love; soulmate love and connection.

Me: It's hard without him here…

Sandra: He is still here and you're definitely going to meet up in the next life. Karma has been cleared. You're going to be fine. Your life is going to bloom.

Me: Is Nick going to be okay?

Sandra: He needs to come to more peace of mind.

Me: He's worried about me.

Sandra: He need not worry. You're living a very long life, and you're going to be very happy.

Grieving someone in death who betrayed you in the most profound way is a burden that only those who have experienced it can understand. Forgiveness is part of my journey in grief, and although I always forgave Joe for everything in his life, his death was not as easy.

The paradox of love and loss is buried deep within my heart and soul and ached like a gaping wound, desperate to find the key to happiness. How I missed having the old Joe beside me.

Rich or poor, ugly or beautiful, wise or unwise, grief is an inescapable journey for having loved and lost someone deeply, profoundly and above all, unconditionally.

Mediumship Meetup and Reading from Anaya - September 2015

As I came to realize that the reason for Joe's suicide was more of an accident than a cold betrayal against our love, I struggled to find forgiveness for this irreversible tragedy. It seemed as though Joe had some kind of 'heart attack of the brain', that he was in a sense impaired from the accumulation of sleep deprivation and stress.

Another evening that September I also went to a Mediumship Meet up. It was run by a Medium named Nora who experienced a tragic loss herself and this led to her career as a Medium. I felt called to attend and didn't know anyone there. I had spoken with Nora on the phone about a reading but decided it was more suitable to gain skills as a Medium myself. I had lots of input from Joe and it was time to test my own abilities.

As I drove to the Meet up and past the cemetery where Joe is buried, I turned the radio on and once again the George Michael song *Father Figure* came on the radio. It seemed I was hearing this song up to a few times a day for the last couple of weeks and I was beginning to suspect Joe had something to do with it. This time, instead of changing the station away from this song I never particularly liked, I listened to the lyrics, wondering what the message was. The whole song struck me as meaningful words coming from Joe's heart, but the words that struck me most were, *"Greet me with the eyes of a child, heaven is a kiss and a smile, Just hold on, I won't let you go, my baby... I will be the one who loves you until the end of time."*

I said to Joe in that moment, "If you say the words, *'Father Figure'* tonight, that is my sign, I know then this is you. That will be my confirmation."

When I arrived on that warm September evening, I was a little nervous. It was in a community centre and I was one of the last of about 8 people to arrive. There was a spot on the sofa beside a beautiful dark-haired woman with large pretty hazel eyes. She had beautiful East Indian features and I immediately felt a connection to her, knowing Joe would have noticed her beauty because there was something special about her. I could see it in her eyes, she was a special soul.

After we settled in we began to practice psychometry. We took a piece of paper and wrote our name on it, folded it, and placed it in a basket. Then we each drew one paper and held it without looking at the name. Each of us 'read' the paper for someone else in the group without a clue of who we were reading or knowing anything about the other people's deceased loved ones.

We each went around explaining our visions and I picked up on an older woman that I thought was somebody's grandmother. The beautiful woman next to me, Anaya read to us without us knowing who the message was for. She described a man who was very tall and handsome.

Here is what Anaya said: "This person who is on the other side is telling their loved one to be more sexy; more showy, and have more 'wow' factor.

They are showing me a red, flashy, 1940's sports car to represent this. It's so shiny. This person should be doing this for their new life with a fresh start. He was the strong, silent type."

She continued, "Oh my, he's very tall with dark hair and very handsome. He's giving me the words 'father figure'."

I could hardly contain myself as she continued, but I wasn't allowed to say anything.

Anaya began to cry, "He says he's very sorry. I'm feeling he has a lot of remorse about his death. He's holding a baby. He says he's got the baby with him. The baby is very young, very tiny. He feels like somebody's father, he keeps saying 'father figure'. He's so sorry about his death. He keeps saying he's sorry and asking for forgiveness. He's saying, 'please forgive me'."

Anaya became overwhelmed with my husband's emotion and by then she was looking at me, knowing this person had suicided. She looked at me as if to want to ask me something personal but not for others to see. She cupped her hands around her mouth, and slowly moved her lips, "Was it a suicide?" I nodded 'Yes', while the facilitator urged me to tell the deceased loved one that he was forgiven.

"I can't say its okay, you're forgiven." I tried to explain. "He hurt me really badly, you don't understand, it's not that easy." I felt like a school girl being urged to forgive her classmate for pulling her hair. This wasn't a simple hurt I was holding onto. She was telling me to forgive someone for causing the death of my loved one. Joe had caused such pain, and he should have known better as my husband, lover and soulmate.

Anaya became more emotional and after the meeting we talked privately. Coincidentally it was World Suicide Prevention Day and Anaya told me she had lost somebody very close to her to suicide as well. She told me she had just declared to the universe that very day that if she were going to do mediumship readings, she was willing to read from deceased loved ones who had died by suicide.

I was stunned at the events that night that brought forth emotion and healing. Joe had chosen this beautiful woman to communicate with me, and I met another beautiful soul on my journey of healing. The power of our deceased loved ones in aiding our healing can be incredible. I know that Joe was listening to me and once again he was reaching out through other special people to help me heal.

I learned that forgiveness is a journey that comes from deep within. Forgiveness is not easily granted like a gift, and true forgiveness comes from deep in the soul of those who are hurt. Sometimes forgiveness evolves and grows like a rose that takes months to blossom on a vine. Other times, like God forgives us, we forgive others without even being asked from our loving divine compassion. Neither is better, it is the journey of the soul that matters.

Chapter 12

In the Arms of the Angels

"Death makes angels of us all and gives us wings where we had shoulders smooth as ravens claws." ~ Jim Morrison

Angel Guidance and Healing Workshop, November 2015

I was lead to take an Angel Guidance and Healing Practitioner course after further discovering the healing power of angels in my bereavement. Just six months after Joe's death I enrolled in this weekend workshop the November after Joe's death.

Joe's spirit was with me the entire time, continuing the healing journey alongside me. Although it was an intensely emotional weekend, I felt safe and loved with the profound company of angels and the support of the other participants in the group. That weekend, a deeply spiritual level of healing took place for all of us. Never before did I feel like I had a little slice of heaven on earth. The energetic frequency was very high and very pure. We were bathed in heavenly, angelic light as all of us held space for one another with the respect of divine beings.

That Saturday morning we did a meditation whose purpose was to dissolve *vows* that could be holding us back in our lives. These could also include past life vows such as vows of poverty and chastity, or present life vows such as marriage vows after divorce. I didn't feel like I had any issues surrounding vows which were holding me back in life, and I reluctantly

Beloved, I Can Show You Heaven

wanted to dissolve my marriage vows to Joe. Nonetheless, I trusted the angels to remove from me what was no longer serving me and always kept an open mind.

When we spread ourselves out for meditation one of the leaders in training, Mary began to take notes. Given my auditory sensitivity, this was intensely distracting to me in the silent room. I didn't like the sound of the pen on paper and found it difficult to concentrate. The group leader, Chris reassured me that once I was in meditation it would fall away and to let it be. As I surrendered into the meditation, Mary stopped writing and she began the meditation also. This allowed me to concentrate better on my thoughts during the guided meditation. Mary approached me after the guided meditation. She received profound visions from someone. She had been guided by spirit to stop writing and also meditate with us.

After the guided meditation was over, Mary was excited to shared with us what had happened to her and she was also excited to privately share with me in more detail what my husband had said to her. The first break after that was the opportunity. We quietly and quickly stole away to a small room and she told me what my husband had said. She said if he could, he would remove what he had done in a heartbeat.

While she was in meditation, my husband appeared to her. He said that he wanted me to 'find peace and be free from all negativity'. He wanted me to feel the incredible peace he felt in heaven.

Joe asked her, "Can you clear vows for the deceased? I am hoping that all vows be released from me, I want to go in peace." Mary told me that he is in intense love and peace. She said that my husband asked me to, 'Talk to the children about the good times now'. Archangel Michael appeared as well as Archangel Jophiel, surrounded in beautiful pink light to disseminate our marriage vows. This was to give me freedom and peace in my soul for the remainder of my incarnation without Joe.

Later on that day, Chris, the teacher was talking about tragic prophecy. I wondered about my own terrible tragedy of Joe's death and why the angels didn't warn me. I remembered the mediumship reading from April 29, 2015, two weeks before Joe's death. During this reading, my son Joseph came to me and said "Daddy and you will find peace". To me in hindsight, my son's words were a prophecy of my husband's death, but until the workshop, my son's words only made sense six months after his dad's death. I thought that maybe I was just beginning to experience that peace.

However, I could not help but think if maybe I understood what those words from my son meant six months prior, that I could have prevented Joe's tragic suicide. At the next break, Mary said to me, "You were thinking something during that lecture, and your husband said, 'Don't even go there'."

Joe used to say, "Don't even go there," when I would say things that were leading down a negative or destructive path, as if to stop my ideas because he knew where I was going before I had a chance to fully verbalize my thoughts. Joe knew I was starting to blame myself for not heeding my son's words that told me, *"Daddy and you will find peace."* Joe was saying not to even think to myself that I could have stopped his death based on what my son had said to me.

At the end of that day, we did another beautiful meditation before going home for the evening. I do not remember the purpose of the meditation but it resulted in an emotional reunion with Joe. I went home and wrote every detail I could remember down. Here is what it said:

I got my wings today. They are beautiful and feel so right. I feel like an Earth angel. My wings are long and fixed between my shoulder blades. They are white with hues of grey.

Joe brought them to me. He said he was so proud of me. He said I would do great, he said I would do awesome. Then he pulled my hands up and we flew together into the clouds of the blue sky. He told me he loved flying, "It is awesome, I love it."

Next, he brought me to the first level of heaven. He was so happy to be able to bring me there. We talked about our son, Joseph. He said, "He looks so much like you. He's so beautiful; he has your nose exactly."

Joe said, "Joseph has been busy like me, always helping people. He helped babies and kids cross to heaven just like you said he would. He helped you with your book; he was there for Nicholas and the girls when they were small. He's busy now, but he'll be around. He has helped me around here (heaven)."

After that, Joseph arrived. I heard his voice so clear. He had angel wings like mine. I noticed that Joe did not have angel wings. Joseph and I talked about all the cool things he has done, and I learned a lot about him. We talked about the signs he had given me after his death, and how I was not ready for the same things to be done with his Dad. I asked for him to help his Dad to be clear with me in his communication from the other side.

That weekend I learned that the protective colours I placed in my aura were visible to others in the group. Most notably, the pink light of love and compassion I surrounded myself with.

At the end of the weekend, a sacred angel walk ceremony was held. We stood facing each other in partners and took turns in a procession saying beautiful messages from the angels to one another. Because of the odd number of participants in the group, I was the only one without a partner and for a moment I felt that Joe was my invisible partner in spirit. When at last it was my turn to take the walk, Chris told me that "Joe is here and he is with you surrounding you with love and encouragement." Chris continued talking to me purely from his intuition, "Someone here has a message for you that is really going to stand out as very important to you. You will know when you hear it, pay attention to what they say."

As I walked down the sacred procession, a woman named Evelyn I had met only once many months before, said to me, "*Congratulations, you've earned your angel wings. When you need courage, remember to put them on, they are beautiful rainbow coloured wings.*"

This was the message that stood out and I won't forget because it reminded me of the meditation the night before where Joe granted me my angel wings and flew me to heaven to meet our son.

Chapter 13

Rose Petals from Heaven

"To love someone deeply gives you strength. Being loved by someone deeply gives you courage." ~ Lao Tzu

As Sandra and I became friends, Joe took the opportunity to communicate through her from heaven. She told me that Joe was becoming my guide but I was still sceptical. I still thought writing this book and connecting with Joe required outside help with an experienced medium, but Sandra insisted that if I released guilt and healed with forgiveness, I would open up more psychically. She told me that Joe was waiting for me to start automatic writing and that when I am ready, everything would flow to me directly through Joe.

Heading into the first winter without Joe, I had a powerful dream. He was very distant in my dreams still and one night I dreamed he had gone away from me for intense therapy which was initiated with the help of the Council of Elders. Joe was in a type of solitary confinement which seemed in some way like a test. He was working on matrixes which were like a machine or piece of equipment. The algorithm would change to a new matrix once he did something correctly. He was not given any help or clues. The purpose of this was to change his thinking to productive and helpful, while eliminating sub-conscious thought patterns which had caused emotional wreckage and frustration in life.

He wasn't allowed to get upset and frustrated. There was no room for error. He had time to figure things out, but he could not get mad if things got too difficult. The matrixes could only be solved if he remained calm and stable. It was meant to prepare him for being my guide, to teach him patience, peace and love at all times without impulsivity. If he couldn't handle it and cope, he would not be permitted to be my guide. Joe was determined and I could see him concentrating on tasks as if he was the mechanic he was in his life, working on a machine or an engine. He was focused and I don't think he was aware that I saw this. He had all of the determination he had in life but at the same time, he was being taught to persevere without expressing frustration or negative emotion.

When I woke, I had to make sense of what I had witnessed, without explanation. I realized my guides were showing me this important step in Joe's evolution on the other side.

I remember when Hope was about two years old I was told in a dream that my grandmother, whose also one her spirit guides, was taking a course the week we were on vacation in Myrtle Beach. I dreamed that in the pool area of the resort another elderly woman told me this. That week Hope would run ahead of us often. One evening, when walking on the busy boardwalk Hope said she 'was going to live with her grandma in heaven' because she didn't like to be scolded for running from us when we were trying to protect her. Joe was on a similar kind of training sabbatical to be the guide for me he wanted to be.

I think that becoming my spirit guide brought Joe peace and satisfaction in turning the results of his unintentional suicide around. From all I have learned and experienced in life, I believe that every negative action can easily be forgiven and healed, but murder and suicide is more difficult because it is the irreversible end of life in a body. Often suicides are very aware when they find themselves conscious but not with a body on the other side. They realize the horrific mistake they made as they realize their death did not end their pain, but precipitated someone else's tragic suffering from their decision to end their life.

Few suicides become soul guides. Many must return quickly to the Earth plane, especially if this is not their first time completing suicide. They often return with even more challenging lives in order to evolve their souls. There are also suicides who are victim souls who are highly evolved. In this sense, suicide is a possibility in their divine soul contract with another highly evolved soul in order to teach the planet about an aspect of healing of life on Earth.

Jennifer Angelee

For example, a young woman who is a victim of sexual assault and abuse, who is traumatized and dies by suicide to escape the shame becomes a reminder of the harm that sexual assault causes, and her parent might become an advocate in speaking out against sexual violence. Both are highly evolved souls who use this experience as an opportunity to help others.

One day in early December, just seven months after Joe died; I decided to take an automatic writing session with Simona Daniels, an energy healer. I thought maybe this was going to be the first step in connecting with Joe in this way. What I learned is, I didn't really need anybody to teach me, I just had to be open to the idea of it and sit with pen to paper. On the way to this automatic writing teaching session, I distinctly remember the ache in my wrist before I arrived. When I began writing, it was if I was a race horse coming out of the starting gate. At the word 'Go' I was like a student writing an intensely timed exam answer after studying and being well-prepared.

Joe was anxious to speak to me through my writing that day in December, just seven months after his death. Here is what was written:

Truth, love, inspiration, patience, practice.

Love, we are here to love, to be the divine for others when they forget who they are, who they came to be, and what we are here for. You are that love for me – thank you!

I need to thank you for being the awesome person that you are with me, for your beauty, your silliness, your fun. You have a light in your eyes like no other I have seen before.

Remember your light, carry it forth, I believe in you; your light, your beauty, your divinity.

You are so special. I have loved you always and forever.

Thank you for the most beautiful children. Thank you for Nicholas –he is so beautiful. Thank you for our angel Faith. Thank you for my little princess Hope.

God love you, you've been through so much. Nothing could ever prepare you for this; that is why you were not prepared. You would have freaked out. I had to end it fast.

My beauty, I miss holding you tight, I miss your touch. Oh I miss your touch more than you miss mine.

You felt like an angel. I was so lucky to have you as my very own earth angel. I should have listened to you, you were right.

Please understand I was so flawed before I met you. My family upbringing was difficult, I resisted but the fight got the better of me. I was human and did not have your high vibration qualities- the ability to know and act with self-love. I was defeated because they were in my mind, in my beliefs.

"Free your mind." I wouldn't do this. I thought I couldn't change my mind like you. You're right, you can change your mind, Lol, like a woman. That's another reason I thought woman were better, men are bitter, they don't change. I became what I hated and couldn't change myself; I didn't believe I was worth helping.

You are so different. You know your creative power, make a mistake, learn from it and change.

Tell Me About Heaven?

Heaven is awesome! You can change here; it's so easy for me.

I cry a lot, cry for how foolish I was, cry for my mistakes, cry for the kids, cry for their suffering and yours. I cry when you cry, laugh when you laugh, sad when you're sad.

I want you to feel joy so that I can feel joy. I live on this side vicariously through you. I hear your thoughts like mine, even taste your food, I taste what you taste.

Please show me heaven Jen. Please! Please! Create your Heaven on Earth and I will be happy. Show the world that this is what happens when we die- we empathize with those who love us most dearly.

It's beautiful here, so peaceful. Still when I see beauty there is melancholy in my heart like when you're missing your loved ones.

Can you bring me there? In my dreams?

I will. You're not ready. Your grief holds you in your heart chakra.

Will I meet someone?

Yes, I am waiting for you to be ready for the introduction. I know you want it but you must be alone now to create for yourself. When you have healed and come to peace he will come, but your ducks must be lined up in a row. When you meet him, you can focus on falling in love and being in a relationship.

You're not ready to fall in love yet. You would be confused with your broken heart and make endless comparisons to me. You've never not been in a relationship. Be in a relationship with yourself, love yourself and you will be so irresistible and feel sexy again.

I'm sorry I could not be the spiritual man for you.

I miss you Joe. This is becoming like Conversations with God. Can you tell me more about heaven? How will the book work?

Transcribe the tapes. Start with you, the meaning of life, your inner childhood, then move to me, my struggles, how tough my parents were, my childhood; our fights, my darkness, my light.

How I loved you on Earth, my rose, my beautiful rose. You were picked by God to blossom on Earth. I was your thorns, very much part of you, and I protected you all those years.

What would my life have been like all of the years I had with you, without you?

You would have been sad and empty. I filled you up. I loved you when you couldn't love yourself. I taught you to see your beauty, find your creativity, manifest your material dreams, gave you motherhood for the kids and taught you how lovable you are because I loved you.

I loved you so much, I sacrificed myself for you, so you could love yourself and show the world there is a heaven, and that heaven can be created on Earth.

Heaven is here now? I don't want to go further without you.

I'm not going anywhere my love. You will have a wonderful life, and so will the kids.

My Rose, God picked you to be the beauty in his earthly garden.

Love lives on, even when the roses die, I will still be loving you. When mountains fall into the sea there will still be you and me.

After the automatic writing, Joe continued to communicate with me through Simona.

Simona: He wants you to buy a large sign that says 'JOY'. He said to put it up and not to take it down after Christmas. He says, 'Please Jennifer, do not label yourself, you are more than those labels. If you take courses, just go to have fun. Do not think you are there to learn, you are there to remind yourself. You are not learning anything that you do not know. Do not label yourself with 'Reiki' or all these labels. Do not put yourself in a box with all these labels, he is saying.

Me: He never liked labels.

Simona: Because he knows how painful labels are. He's really laughing and saying, "Don't label yourself. He is saying shred the boxes, be authentic, you are you. So, if people ask you, you may label this, this, this, but you may say I am creating my own because I have an idea." Do you understand? You go somewhere and say I have this, this, this, and you put yourself in someone's labels and you put yourself behind them like a tail. Put yourself first and if you wish, use these labels as a tail…I am an earth angel, and I am channelling this. Somebody channelled Reiki and came up with that, and it's outgrown, perhaps.

Me: I feel like I have outgrown what I have learned so far.

Simona: Then don't identify with it.

Me: The word 'wisdom' came up this morning in my therapy session, and 'compassion'.

Simona: He says, have compassion for yourself and love yourself. He is here; do you want to know anything?

Me: Of course. I am worried about Christmas. It is going to be hard without him.

Simona: He says buy the most beautiful JOY sign and put it up.

Me: I see those signs everywhere when I shop. I don't feel joy…Did we plan his death like this?

Simona: (*softly*) Yes, yes, yes. You made that contract together on a soul level before you met. It was harder for him here than it is for you here, that is what he is saying. He sacrificed himself for you and your children because if he were here you would not be doing what you're doing now. You are expanding, huge, huge.

Me: Can he tell me more about my work?

Simona: Go with the flow. He's showing me a big table of food, beautiful food, fresh, organic. There is a lot on the table for you to eat; you wouldn't be able to eat it all today. You don't plan what you will cook on December 17, 2035. Do you care what you will eat this night?

Me: Oh, no I don't care.

Simona: He is very wise this man. Why do you care about your future? It's beautiful, it's expanding...

Me: Will I always be sad about him?

Simona: If you choose to, yes.

Me: Will I love somebody like I loved him?

Simona: Have you loved yourself where you are in bliss and ecstasy with yourself?

Me: No.

Simona: This is how much he loves you. This is a time for a relationship with your self. You can only love another human being as much as you love yourself. You need to love yourself in this way to make sure you meet that person. Not yet, heal your wounds, you don't want to meet someone when you are sad, when you are not choosing to be happy yet, because then you will meet someone who is sad. Two sad people in a house with your children is not what you want to create.

His body is not here but he is more alive than he ever was. He knows how important it is to create for you and your children. Nobody can make you happy or not happy; you have a choice on a deeper level, to go from your mind to your heart. Every moment is a choice, choose wisely.

You need to give yourself the credit, all these sessions, all that work, you are becoming spiritual. This means becoming authentic. You need to choose joy instead of sorrow, it is a choice. It is not the outside world that creates this. I am seeing a building coming down, the ground shaking. The tower just crashed. The outside system for human beings for the last 2000 years is so limited and it's crashing.

Me: I feel like I am a messenger for that and we need to change the status quo, and he is helping me, and everything that I created that was material for us, has crashed. I feel like everything that was superficial in my life has disappeared, and now I am creating our home to be a spiritual place of love. I want to create an energy flow in the house, in my house where all motivation is out of love and not out of fear. Of course, we cannot be perfect but I ask myself with everything, 'Am I doing this out of love or fear?' Because what we were doing before wasn't working. We were working to achieve things under time constraints, like normal people do, and now I want it to be about the essence and meaning of life, that we don't go to work just to pay the bills. That we do things out of love, trusting that our bills and our finances will be taken care of, that there will be abundance. I feel he is helping even though I'm sad. I am sleeping better than I ever have.

We discussed my numerology and the fact that my first home address actually is the same as my birthday. I told her about the day I was born after my mom was raking the leaves from the tree my Dad planted in 1955, 60 years ago.

Me: When my Dad got home from work, he drove my mom to the hospital and I was born so fast he did not get the opportunity to be there.

Simona: Did you know people who are born very fast are spiritual leaders?

Me: No, I did not.

Simona: Did you know that your husband is master number 22? You are number 3, the third eye. Ten is a soul number, one is beginning, zero is God. Everything comes from nothing. Two is duality, everything is both ways, but when you decide everything is okay, you will be more balanced, there will be less polarity. Because your husband had a master number, he taught you this strong duality, he taught you about that duality, he was this was or that way, black or white.

Me: Yes, he was a black and white thinker. He was more certain of things, he was more judgemental. He either liked you or not. When it came to drinking for example, he would over do it, or nothing at all, whereas I would go out for dinner and have one glass of wine, I could find the balance. He was a workaholic, very determined. He used his will, I was more flowy and from the heart. It's a tough one to get along with, isn't it, 22?

Simona: He could find the balance. It's a beautiful thing. He mastered so many things in his past lives.

Me: He was so talented. He mastered so many things and could manifest.

Simona: Put it together two and two and it is four, a very stable number. He understood things on a deeper level. It's like a chair…

Me: In some ways he was too stable, and became unstable, if that makes any sense? Like a chair, if you take away one leg, it's not stable anymore.

Simona: You have to come from the centre, and with any number, even number three. You use your ability of number three for good will of people. The triangle is the third eye, to tell people, "That is your choice, and you are choosing that because you are choosing to learn from your past and expand." For other people, if something like this would happen, they would go crazy. They would see ghosts, spirits.

Me: I have already experienced all of that stuff and it doesn't scare me now, and it's like 'so what?'

Simona: Now you are experiencing all this communication with him and it is so beautiful because it is meant to be, but you choose that path. Other woman could have ended up on drugs or alcohol, or in a mental hospital.

Me: I had two choices, sink or swim, I chose to swim.

Simona: You can take it from the heart and manifest something or you can go to the mind and it is self-destruction. If you go self-constructive and then you can manifest. You just need your mind to do things like banking, …

Me: My son is a three also.

Simona: Your youngest is four also like your husband, she's very strong. Your older daughter is seven, which is a mystical number. All of your houses are 8. That is the number of infinite possibilities. The energy of your home is easy for you to live on when living with challenges. Your childhood home was ten which is familiar to your energy.

Me: Yes but in that childhood house, there wasn't the challenges.

Simona: In the infinite possibilities, there are solutions to the challenges. The solution is very visible.

Chapter 14

Rose Petals Drop on Fallen Snow

"The sorrow we feel when we lose a loved on is the price we pay to have had them in our lives." ~ Rob Liano

The months after my husband's death, my son and I worked together to figure out some of the physical things around our house. Understandably this was a difficult time for a young man who had been through the traumatic death of his father. It was stressful but he was trying to carry on with living life as normal as possible. He was working far too many hours at his part-time job and he had loads of homework with a full course load of four university level subjects.

Despite the heartache, he pulled through successfully in all ways but things became very difficult for him that Christmas holiday. I felt very helpless as I could not return his father to him. I was exhausted myself and had to create an okay Christmas for the kids with just the four of us. It was sad. My relationships with my siblings were strained, and I had almost no contact with Joe's family.

I did make an effort to have Joe's family over as I sensed from Joe in spirit that this is what he wanted, but they ignored my invitation.

That Christmas Eve, we went to an early mass and then went to my parents for turkey dinner with my brother's family. We had a pleasant dinner, my parents always made the best of Christmas no matter what was going on. I'm proud this trait existed in our family and always wished Joe's family could have these resilient qualities. To me, there seemed to be sadness and conflict in their home. When Joe was alive I often resisted being around his family's home. I felt like I was never approved of no matter what I did.

When we got home, we put on our pyjamas and read our traditional bedtime story, 'Twas the Night Before Christmas' in front of the fire and Christmas tree in the family room.

I played Santa all alone that Christmas Eve. How I missed Joe! Though I always did all the work anyway, he always patiently waited by me, trying to be supportive as he could. I know he was waiting for alone time with me each Christmas Eve, but as soon as I finished, it was close to midnight and I was exhausted, anxious and needed to get to bed for our excited children the next morning.

On Christmas Day the kids were happy and brave. We refused to soak in our sorrow and had an invite to a relative's home. We decided to go, but with an escape clause – the movies. We received an apprehensive reception from some as my family tried nonchalantly to carry on as usual. Some of my family members simply ignored us. A painful part of grieving unfortunately becomes the change in the way that others relate to the grieving. Many people have never had the experience of losing someone very close to them. It's not something one wants to imagine because its scary. Often others choose to ignore it, or in the case of suicide, they subconsciously hold blame those closest to deceased.

We stayed for a short while and just as soon as we were done eating, we left to see *Daddy's Home*, a family comedy with Will Farrell and Mark Wahlberg. The movie was funny but we couldn't escape the absence of our Dad, and it was bittersweet. I sensed Joe at the theatre with us, and it being a story about a stepfather, I wondered if I would ever find somebody to be a stepdad to my kids.

There was one scene in the movie, I knew Joe would think was hilarious, the part where Will Farrell proudly comments on his vehicle, his Ford Flex. Joe and I had a few brief conversations in his living years about this vehicle. Joe liked this vehicle, and each time he brought it up, I soothingly told him, so he wasn't offended, that I thought it was a funny looking car.

When the movie was over, I asked Nicholas his thoughts, and he replied, "It was hard to watch." Nicholas carried on with such strength from the time of Joe's death in May to December, continuing to work and study. When he finally got a chance to rest that first Christmas holiday he spent time lying in bed depressed. I naturally had concerns after what he had been through and so I slept in my daughter's bedroom across the hall from him.

I made a medical appointment for him as soon as he could be seen. At the appointment I read a poster about the brain and depression in the office. It became clear to me that Joe had all the symptoms of depression. I felt it a shame and relief at the same time. A shame that we did not realize something was wrong before it was too late, and a shame that he did not get help.

The relief was because I understood medically that Joe had truly suffered with depression for many years; it wasn't just one momentary lapse of reason, but a lifetime of depression Joe had suffered with. This partially relieved me of some of the guilt I was storing.

Soon after Joe died my Dad had even denied that Joe even had depression, stating, "He was always even keeled and level headed when I saw him". This made me feel like there was no validity in my memories of Joe having depression. It reinforced in me that I was to blame for what Joe did. As I became healthier and stronger, I understood Joe's illness with greater compassion and clarity despite what anyone said.

There were many events from Joe's past that left an unhealed scars on Joe's mind. I felt Joe's pain and sadly, I believe that his past is just one of the factors that led to Joe's depression. Joe had a lot of healing to do, and in hindsight I believe it is worth mentioning because I believe it is so important that each one of us finds peace with our past. Many people experience trauma in their lives, and there is now scientific evidence how this can affect the physiology and chemistry of our brain. It is so important that we take the time to heal the aspects of ourselves that are hurt and in pain. We are not meant to suffer. Suffering is the resistance to healing.

After the first Christmas without Joe, things continued to be difficult and we still missed him terribly, but the kids and I began to heal on a deeper, spiritual level and I began to sense that the energy begin to shift. I believe this was because of the healing that Joe had also done on the other side. He was very much in our home and around the children, and I could sense this presence in a more positive way in day to day life.

I struggled to make peace with the fact that my beloved was no longer physical but gained confidence in myself and my future. When my friend Sandra came for coffee one January morning, I was upset because our little dog was peeing on the hardwood floor in the main hallway of our home, a hallway which runs from the front door to the back door in the kitchen. Sandra said Joe appeared in her car on the way to my home and gave her a message. When she arrived, she was concerned about me and asked if I was okay. He told her that I was going to be great and told me to have a great trip.

Sandra asked when she arrived, "Are you going away?"

I had just booked a vacation with the kids to Barbados during March Break. I told her how upset I was about the dog's accidents and she said, "You know dogs are psychic, they see things. Joe is walking in the hall every morning and Buster sees him."

Sandra's explanation made perfect sense but it didn't solve the problem of my dog's accidents from the excitement of seeing his former master. I told Joe, "I am glad you are here to visit us, but do me a favour, don't walk in the halls, do what it takes, go through the walls or whatever you need to figure out in spirit." Fortunately, soon after, there was a remarkable improvement in Buster's accidents.

Joe and I had begun communicating with greater ease from the other side. As Joe found peace in heaven, I was adapting to a new life without him using the ability to communicate with Joe on a higher level in everyday life.

Chapter 15

My Ascended Beloved

"So close, no matter how far, couldn't be much more from the heart. Forever, trust in who we are, and nothing else matters." ~ Metallica

Hungry to learn more about where my husband was on a spiritual level, I booked a phone reading with a Medium I had met at a Meet Up. It was not the greatest reading and I am only mentioning it because I want others to know that not all Mediums are wonderful and not all readings are positive. This man told me my husband was unhappy in the shadow realms and that I needed to pack up all his stuff, let him go and move on with my life. He left me worried and confused and what he said contradicted the healing that had taken place over the first nine months. Therefore I booked a reading with Carol Righton soon after and this proved to be a profound reading with amazing insight:

Reading on Unity Consciousness with Carol Righton February 19, 2016

Carol: Interesting though, you are working with Archangel Michael at this time, his energy is coming through right now. So what do I mean by that? His energy is connecting to your soul guides, and he's communicating with your soul guides. Do you understand what that means? And he's showing me protection for you, everything is safe for you. Also they are the holy liberators releasing you from constraints, restrictions. They are helping you release and strengthen your consciousness.

Me: Mmm. I really am. I have lots of questions…I will start with something light for my husband: should I buy a new vehicle now?

Carol: I heard 'yes' right away, he said it's time for you to let go and not hang on, and he said it's time for something new for you. He's giving you gratitude too. He's sending you gratitude; do you understand what that is? I think because you've really moved forward.

Me: He usually doesn't.

Carol: He doesn't? Well today he is sending gratitude, feel your heart!

Me: (Tears coming) Yeah, he's almost crying and he's saying 'thank you', thank you. You're doing great Hun.' Where is he, is he,…? I heard…

Carol: Oh, stop listening to people and start coming into your own! One of the things he's saying is: you need to trust yourself more and listen to your messages. He's saying you've been getting a lot of conflicting, unanswered messages and he says there is not quite the clarity, and he says with your guardians is to *listen* to yourself. He says not to surrender your power away or over, and to see your abilities. Yeah! You can feel it. Now you tell me, you ask him, feel him, how he's doing…feel it.

Me: I feel it. I feel the energy; my heart to his heart. He's crying but he's releasing tears of joy, um, the times he showed me appreciation he cried, he was often just emotional with gratitude. That means it's him.

Carol: I want you to acknowledge things right now. I know you've been told some things. Acknowledge it. He is saying THIS IS TRUTH. THIS, RIGHT NOW!

He says, 'She is not telling you what to feel, she is holding space, right now, feel it, sense it, know it, this is truth!"

Okay? It can get a little confusing out there because everyone defines the messages in their own way. That is why I say, 'you feel it' because everyone's messages are communicated in a way that they understand. He's actually saying that you've grounded in again and you feel it. Feel it. (Laughing) Oh he feels so much better, doesn't he?

Me: He must be okay because I've healed so much.

Carol: Feel him, does he feel okay?

Me: Yeah, he feels awesome.

Carol: Yeah! Like what a difference!

Me: I couldn't be as well as I am if he was in the shadows.

Carol: Nooo, he's doing great. Very good, and he's in gratitude to you.

Me: So I don't need to send him to the light and stuff.

Carol: He's already there, feel it. I'm really proud of him. I'm proud of you and him. You've both done your work, congratulations! It has wings, feel it in your cells.

Me: When I got here the singing bowl made me shift.

Carol: I knew you were going to make it. You are very good at what you do; I don't want people to take that away from you. You hear the messages, you feel, you know, you sense. And it's interesting because right now, I'm seeing behind you a fabric, like when the wind blows but its actually light coming from you. And it's interesting because the colours are like tie-dye, but only brighter. You have this huge fabric, that is how energy shifts, it looks like fabric. You are doing good rainbow work, I have to say.

Me: What do you mean rainbow work? I've been using rainbows in my ideas, my illustrations. That is my theme.

Carol: See, what you are seeing, feeling, sensing and knowing is you are sitting in your aura, your light body. Your light body is actually merging into you. You are becoming your light body. You are not as dense anymore, we're crystallizing.

Me: I feel that. I feel 'Clair', like such clarity in everything that happens to me. I just cut through all the BS. I just feel and know, and I think I am so much different than I used to be.

Carol: You are so awesome!

Me: (laughing) Oh, thank you! I am ascending, my energy is ascending.

Carol: And what does ascension mean to you?

Me: (pause) Just that my frequency, like at my soul level is what it is meant to be, so I am not coming from an egocentric place. I am free from my ego, like a snake sheds its skin, and I've just slithered out. (*Laughing*)

Carol: Interesting analogy. The snake represents consciousness. Ascension is consciousness. The unity within you is now ready to merge with the consciousness of the planet.

Me: Unity Consciousness. I've been writing about that for the book. I wrote the afterward which is about Unity Consciousness and from that word, I wrote it.

Carol: Where are you getting it?

Me: I am merging with the unity; I'm finding I am aware of everything, doing what you said in Reiki. I am just kind of walking, opening the door, seeing what's inside. It's like walking in a forest and there are different paths and each one is a delight.

Carol: Awesome.

Me: Yeah, and my house is a mess, and I don't care that much (laughs).

Carol: That will shift when it's ready. Hey, when you start and channel and write, all time disappears, and you look at the time and it flies. There is no separation. You are not in third dimension consciousness, you are right in the fifth, and walking in first, second and third and helping other people transcend.

Me: Okay, I read about that in Theta Healing. Am I from the fifth dimension, bringing those in third to the Source?

Carol: Absolutely. We're holding space for them. Wherever you are, you're holding space for them, there is DNA communication. That is why you are having a hard time with concept of time because everywhere you look you're in the space of communion and communication with the unity consciousness.

Me: Yes, I am often late, I lose track of time.

Carol: You can ask them to come to you when you have time, or you cannot worry about mundane time. Each day and time will represent something different.

Me: I have a big question now with Joe. Was this supposed to happen? My understanding is with a soul contract, it's known as a possibility that some people will depart by suicide, and then there are opportunities for the people who are left behind. So the pathways are lit up and new opportunities appear. But was he supposed to die like this? To me it's a little bit unique. This is not your typical…

Carol: Absolutely. This is not your regular suicide. I get a lot of these passings and it is not typical, it's a very fascinating energy actually.

Me: A friend of mine says that Joe is actually more evolved than me, but we're going to ascend together when I die. I actually came up with this myself; he is actually a guide for me, or will be a guide for me and others in my work.

Carol: I am going to ask you one question: Do you think your consciousness of unity is merging now?

Me: Like at this moment in my life?

Carol: Do you think that your consciousness, of unity, is merging, together, now?

Me: (pause) Yes.

Carol: Absolutely. You're already ascending. What does ascension mean? Expanding of consciousness. Your consciousness' have already merged together. You are together in consciousness now, in unity.

Me: Was that meant to be? Was it contracted that way?

Carol: I've been studying DNA Therapy and we all come in with certain codes, and when there is a certain combination, it can happen, they can suicide. There is a certain code consciousness. Was it meant to be? We always have free will here. (Pause, listening to Joe) Thank you, he says that's the one thing that keeps hooking you into third dimensional consciousness. What do you think?

Me: I know if he stayed I would not be where I am…

Carol: That's what he says. He says there is more unity with you two right now than there ever was with him being in the physical body. Interesting enough, his physical body was more in control than his soul body.

Me: Uh-huh. He was a very physical person, and had incredible strength. My nephew said he had the strength of ten men. He was a machine. In some ways, it's such a waste, such a shame because what an amazing physical specimen he was and he was so handsome and everything. I really miss that.

Carol: Yes, I know, you're missing the touch, the physical connection. But interesting, he's saying when he was here; you were missing a spiritual connection. Now he's saying you're having both, you're now having my spiritual. He's showing me that you two have merged consciousness. You two have merged the soul expansion of yourselves.

Me: I couldn't have that when he was alive and it was killing me how I tried.

Carol: It was non-productive, it wasn't pushing you. He's saying you weren't contractually moving forward. Neither of you were moving forward. (To Joe) How do you explain this? Explain this to her in a way that she'll understand. Explain this to her. Remember we're human, trying to make sense. We have human bodies; we have human thoughts, so try to communicate this to us in a way that we, in our human essence can understand... (Pause).

He says this is about family expansion. He says that this is about family consciousness. He says that you're receiving the enlightening, you are receiving the wisdom. He says it's about releasing the concepts; it is all about releasing the human concepts.

Me: When he's talking about family, I don't think he's just talking about our kids, he's talking about our extended family. Some family was very like, 'Why the hell did this happen?' and they had lots of existential questions.

Carol: Yeah, he's saying there are perceptions which keep getting in the way of our expansion of realization, is what he is saying. He's saying 'There is such a *limited*, they are so limited in their human concept of spirit, and spirituality and the soul; how we are not separated'. You are working with him! You are breaking the concept, breaking the barrier, piercing the perception of our mundane thinking. You are creating the expansion of conscious-ness! And you are showing the reality that there is an expansion of unconditional love that can come from this experience, when we stop judging, when we stop categorizing, when we stop trying to pinpoint it in all these degrees of separation. He says: Separation is killing our planet. It is creating separation in each of us, and he says with this separation, it is keeping us in pain. It is keeping us in low vibration thinking. He says he passed because this is the unity consciousness speaking between both of you. You merged together as one. He says there is no such thing! He's breaking it; he's piercing the vein of this concept.

He says that humans have the right to move in and out of all dimensions when we feel called. Wow!!! (Laughing)

Me: He could never express it, but whenever I had an ah-ha moment he would say, 'Yeah, absolutely, that's right.' He knew, but he just didn't articulate it. He was not an ignorant person. He was smart. He was an awesome manifestor, he was so gifted.

Carol: And he's still manifesting. Right as we speak! He's breaking the barriers. He's saying 'Don't let them create limits on you.' He says you are merging, you are fifth dimension; fifth dimension doesn't separate. Every time you separate your thinking, every time you think of shame, guilt, or you think of, ah…He says, "Oh, that is just a concept that the third dimension has created to create limits on every human beings capacity to communicate with divinity"…Wow! (Laughs)
He's putting it beautifully, isn't he?

Me: Yeah, and I feel such a voice in me, and I was the shyest kid and teenager in high school and Joe was too shy to talk to me.

Carol: If I were to ask you what colour ray he is, what would you say?

Me: Oh, well I saw yellow when you were asking the question.

Carol: It is, it's gold, I understand why you saw yellow. He is standing in gold. Absolute gold! Gold is one of the highest frequencies.

Me: Like the *Stairway to Heaven* song, 'Everything turns to gold'.

Carol: What he is teaching right now is our perception of separation. He says when we process and analyze things, he says 'separation is the devil'. Analyzing is the negative energy, the minute we start to analyze in a non-productive way and put things into categories; it drops our vibration frequency into third dimension. He says we're in fifth. How do we become fifth beings? He says we become fifth beings by recognizing and not separating.

Me: I understand those who have analytical minds. I'm just going to go out and buy that car and not analyze.

Carol: Good for you! Em-power baby. Empower! Interesting because he's saying let her feel, pay attention to your crown.

Me: Hmm! Wow. It's like whuusht!

Carol: Feel how big it is right now? He's opened the crown. That's divinity's communication. He's saying don't limit yourself by the awe, the God. He's talking about we are all one galactically; there are many, many beings of light. Keep channelling; he's got a lot to show you. Feel it, feel that he is alright, feel it in your hands. Feel the presence of him in the gold light, breathe it in.

Me: I feel it in my solar plexus. It's so strange, I am such an anxious worrier but I just feel like I have nothing to worry about anymore...

Carol: Isn't it amazing. We're free. We're free of the constraints of separating. He says, "Speak your language, speak, be who you are, because if we're not who we are, how are we ever going to shatter the frequency of low consciousness, of third dimension reality." He says third dimension reality is the one that is separating, that says I've got to have the bigger house, I've got to have the bigger car. It is the realities of shame, guilt, anger, judgement, he says release it all because that is not fifth dimension. He says you're meant to move through this universe, this dimension, this planet with the recognition and realization of the consciousness of the unity of the fifth dimension and more, reality. That's how he's speaking. He's got it good now.

I really feel in this instance, from what I've studied about this, that we just check out, but it is our perception that brings it into a non-beneficial reality. He says that all humans have the right to check in and out. In your case, it just feels like such service to me. Both of you have agreed on this service, and that you are actually not separated, but you are united. You are united.

He showed me when he said 'united', it was a flame, and he showed me a flame.

Me: It is like Pentecost. It reminds me of Pentecost. Remember when the Holy Spirit comes? After Easter?

Carol: It feels like the heart flame of consciousness, the universal consciousness of universal love.

Me: I feel it too, so how could it just be him?

Carol: I feel like for me, you two are not separated at all. You are on a physical level. I understand, but he's actually offered you both.

Me: Will I ever have a physical relationship with somebody else?

Carol: If you want, he says. He hopes that for you because he says when you share physically, he shares physically. He hopes for that for you. Now, it's funny he's showing me a flame, eh?

Me: I feel so ascended, I worry I'm not going to find another person that's at a high vibration.

Carol: It will be your choice. He wants you to understand that he is open to it because when you experience it, so does he, so there is no separation. There is no separation in consciousness. He says when you analyze it in the third dimension you're going to say, 'Am I being fair?' He says no, you must start analyzing everything on a fifth. Fifth means part of the energy in his soul is within your soul. That is the expansion, and actually your souls have actually expanded into one consciousness now. Do you get it?

Me: Hmmm, kind of.

Carol: So, if we all come from source, think of each one of us as a cell. If all our cells come out of source, aren't we all one? He says that you've moved your energy field into divinity consciousness, so how would that separate you from him?

Me: Right, so we're meeting in the Source. We are not meeting on a physical level. Oh wow.

Carol: Isn't that fascinating, he says we're all Source, so that is why you want to expand your consciousness out. That is ascension. That means that all consciousness is meeting in source. All of us are meeting in Source, even in a physical body. So then there is no veil, isn't that amazing? (Drawing concentric circles on paper as she explains)

Me: Yes, I feel like there is no veil at all now, let alone seeing him on the other side of the veil.

Carol: He's merged in because you have now ascended to Source. He is already in Source. You are Source in a physical body. You have merged with him.

Me: That is pretty neat, I am Source in a physical body, yeah, and I keep saying to myself in a non-arrogant way, that I am God.

Carol: We all are.

Me: Yes, but I feel it.

Carol: So do I, so I don't think there is anything wrong with that. He is actually showing us. He is actually showing us, the more we expand our perception, the more Source grows. (While drawing larger concentric circles) See how Source is growing? It's actually growing and expanding.

Source, with our consciousness expands, into one, and becomes unity because we're all encompassing in one.

Me: Wow. (Laughing) He's pretty good.

Carol: (laughing) That's pretty cool. (Changes to goofy voice) Well thanks for coming!

Me: (laughing) He's laughing. He was very modest but a ladies man.

Carol: That's why the gold. Feel it.

Me: I see a halo, a golden halo – the golden halo!

Carol: That's why they're doing it. That's the energy of divine.

Me: Those concentric circles reminded me of a nucleus. I was listening to Bruce Lipton the other day and he was talking about the atomists and the materialists? The atomists believe there is actually energy in an atom that is not physical that you cannot explain, so that is the part where I believe energy healing takes place because if you put the energy in the atoms you can change things.

Carol: That is why they show us sacred geometry, the tree of life, the flower of life, the seed of life. Actually what I am working on with you now is sacred geometry. All things come out of source but right now they are expanding it for me.

Me: Hmmm. Is Nicholas going to be okay?

Carol: It's tough. With my son I prayed to Mother Mary.

Me: I am trying to get my son to change his perception. He is still sweating over his marks but I'm pretty sure he's in the program he wants and I told him that.

Carol: Okay, that is old cell memory and communication. Even when he's past it, he still has to train the cells; they will bring up that memory and create the anxiety in the body. There is so much separation in the planet also that what is happening in these kids is it is causing anxiety within them.

College is going to be better for him than high school because high school is about separation.

Me: And they are also moving into their souls plan, be it illustration, or computers for Nicholas. He will be doing what he is here to do and being true to himself, and they all are, hopefully.

Carol: The shift is taking place. As you move forward, the expansion of your family is moving forward, so have faith in that. Fear and worry will create separation.

Me: He worries me so much.

Carol: First of all, he might not even have the codes to do what his father did. It's a great possibility he doesn't even have the codes.

Me: I think he is more like me.

Carol: He is more like you.

Me: He can have the feelings but he stops and thinks of what he has to look forward to.

Carol: He has to have the code. Honestly, some combinations are so hard and they have a check out point. There is nothing wrong with that. It is the perception of our thought that is creating the pain, our thought, what we are being told. We are being told something that is not truth.

Me: So Joe had the nature, and he had the nurture, and he had the circumstance to do what he did?

Carol: Plus he had a purpose; his is to break the perception of this, what we are talking about, suicide, because we have it in the wrong view, in the wrong light. And those who suicide are actually holding themselves in lower consciousness when they can actually just expand into Source. So this is about breaking all barriers.

Me: So the idea that suicides stay in the shadows is because of their perception of what they did? Ooooh! Okay, that makes sense to why Joe is where he is.

Carol: So with most suicides they take on such hard vibration energies and usually check out to re-organize and come back. With your husband, it's very different, he's doing something unique, and so will he wait for you? Yes, he is trying to show through you that it is our perception that is creating the void. Perception is creating the pain.

Me: And I know his problems were only the perception of the problem, they really weren't that bad. The experiences I had with that person blaming me; she said it would not have happened if I weren't like that…, that's all the perception.

Carol: Absolutely, they are doing third dimension energy, and he says that is exactly the kind of barrier we have to break.

Me: The reason that happened is so I can overcome. Their words are so third dimensional it carries a physical density.

Carol: Beautiful. See that shows you the density of our thoughts.

Me: And the limitedness. It's almost like a wall. When she said those words she put up a wall in front of herself.

Carol: Absolutely, because she doesn't want to admit she's wrong. That's her code I bet. She doesn't want to admit there is something to what you're saying. How limited are we in third dimension.

Me: She is a good example of how not to be.

Carol: Well she's just showing you an example of limited thinking, how we're separating ourselves from divine consciousness. Our thoughts are keeping us from expanding our consciousness.

Me: It's like Nicholas Copernicus - he realized that the solar system involved the earth revolving around the sun. He kept that information to himself until his death bed so that the church couldn't have him retract his statement or persecute him for that. He released the information on his death bed, and then the church had no alternative but to accept it.

Carol: This is the same situation. This is about piercing the veil of our perception in consciousness and expanding our awareness into the fifth dimension of unity.

Me: My work, my health?

Carol: Okay, so Joe says stop worrying because that causes separation and keeps you from fifth dimension. Manifestation is fifth dimension. Worry lowers the vibration and frequency and consciousness of it. Are you getting that one?

Me: Yup. I know. Just go for it, whatever happens is what I'm meant for in this life.

Carol: One of the things he's saying is that unity consciousness, moving into intelligence means faith, mercy, forgiveness, trust, love, unconditional love, reverence, communion, peace, surrendering, acceptance, he's using the word beauty. He's saying 'all' and that 'I am'. He's saying those are words with high vibrations to focus on.

Me: Wow. Okay, thank you!

Carol: It's interesting because he keeps showing the swirl. That was you (pointing at dot in middle of swirl). That was you and him actually, and now this is you (showing me the larger expanding concentric circles). Again, that's Source, so we are all in the Source, so he's saying words will keep you there. Right? It's more dense.

Me: Soul Evolution is about developing virtue.

Carol: Virtue is another word, put it down. I see you travel for you, speaking, reading your book, reading your book to people, and then signing it.

Me: In the States?

Carol: Everywhere. You can manifest to the size you want and as long as you're in unity with all. Will you be big? Yes, because you are moving into the unity consciousness and you were born to write. You are actually born to write and channel. Are you channelling it? Yes, because you're merging yourself into the fifth, sixth and seventh dimension where there is no separation. He's showing with light, it's beautiful. He's showing me with a pebble, when it goes into the water, its rings expand out.

Me: Aaaah! That would be a great book cover (laughs).

Carol: He's showing me that in rainbows.

Me: Ooh!

Carol: Watch also how it rains and the drops merge together on the window.

Me: I used to watch this when I was a child.

Carol: You've actually merged with your higher self. Stop separating!

Me: How many people that you read are really like that?

Carol: I feel people are really merging and books like that are so positive it will really help people merge. Messages are so profound.

Me: Thank you.

Carol: I want to thank you. I want to thank you for your soul guides, and I especially want to thank your husband for his profound communicating in a way that I understand. As well as my soul guides, angel, archangels and all beings of light. Thank you!!
And *thank you*. It was a real honour.

Me: That was better than Long Island Medium (laughing). We should have had a TV camera in here.

Carol: In these sessions, everyone expands.

Me: Yeah that's awesome!

This was an exceptionally profound reading with a powerful message that is beyond personal. Not only did I begin to grasp the concept of merging into Source with my beloved, I learned how it is possible that we can all merge with Source in a physical body.

Joe eloquently explained Unity Consciousness beyond a mere theory but as proof that we are all one. I had written about this briefly in my first book *Miracles of Love, Faith and Hope*, but I was applying it to the density of third dimensional reality and the challenges that face us through separation and the healing power of inclusiveness. Throughout modern history is the story of separation. Separation through war, through famine, discrimination, prejudice, slavery, rich and poor, class systems, hierarchy, religion, exploitation, colonialism, racism, and so on. These words carry very low vibration frequency.

As humanity awakens to a rebirth of consciousness, the age of intuition, we recognize our spiritual nature and understand we are more than our minds, our bodies and our social systems. We become conscious and aware of who we are without the external constructs that we used traditionally to define ourselves. We are *the* 'I am', the being; not the, "I am who you say I am (labels) or the 'doing'."

Scientifically we now understand the properties of energy that are not physical. We are divine, just as everything is divine, and of divinity.

Joe points out that as we ascend our energy, by negating labels and being who we are, living in truth, and connecting into the fifth, sixth and seventh dimension (Source), we are merging into the oneness of all that is.

His explanations were very impressive and beyond a usual mediumship reading. It is especially impressive for a man who had difficulty expressing what he knew while in a physical body. Joe was fascinated by physics and if he had the opportunity to attend university in his life, I always knew his degree would be in Physics. I never would have guessed, however, he would be channelling information based on unity consciousness and quantum physics to me from the other side.

This reading was incredibly healing to me both on a personal level and on an expanded level. Typical mediumship readings usually serve to heal the bereaved in their grief; to bring closure and messages of love and hope. Joe's reading, however, pierced the illusion of the veil of separation between the dead and the living.

It is possible to ascend and merge into your light body in a physical body and be united with a deceased loved one on a spiritual level. It's fascinating and I feel empowered in my experience to heal and teach others so that they too can ascend their consciousness.

I have solidified concepts for myself to teach to others. My book, *Stairway to Heaven*, teaches others how to ascend their vibrational frequency in a physical body and raise their consciousness to fifth, sixth and seventh dimensions of existence.

Beloved, I Can Show You Heaven

Looking back to my Kundalini Awakening in 2012, I feel it precipitated the expanded growth that is occurring in my healing. For those of you not familiar with the term Kundalini Awakening, it is the divine energy of Source rising from our Sacral Chakra and involves an awakening of consciousness to Source. As the latent Kundalini ascended through my chakras in 2012, it felt something like an electrical cord having surges of energy pass through it, but the energy remained within my aura, not yet able to plug into a higher consciousness to transcend and process through. Now it is as if I am connected to the oneness of the universe and all energy flows from my crown to Source. My beloved is the conduit.

The other value of this reading is Joe's emphasis on mental concepts that we place on ourselves. Joe wanted to demonstrate how we are limitless beings with infinite potential. He inspired and affirmed for me the importance of living without the constraints of pre-conceived notions and concepts of the society we are born into. God is non-physical, so all of the values and mores of the society in which we live in are a human construct. A poignant example of this is the ideas we place around traditional marriage, the love that takes place between a man and a woman, close in age and of heterosexual orientation for the pro-creation of children. I am not debunking the value of this marriage, and indeed this was the marriage and relationship that Joe and I shared in a physical body. I value and treasure beyond words what we shared, and I would take it back in a heartbeat if I could. But the love we shared was so divine that death did not separate us, or diminish it. In fact, it expanded our love, and each of us ascended and evolved our souls into infinite and unified consciousness with the divine.

Chapter 16

Heaven and Hope

"Signals from spirit may be elaborate or simple but they are always all around us." - James Van Praagh

March 2016

At last I was gaining confidence as a Medium. My confidence increased and it became easier and more natural to read for others. My ego was out of the way, I had been through the worst and I didn't care as much what people thought of me. That was a good thing. I was no longer the self-conscious girl I used to be. Like a snake I shed my skin and the new me slithered out ready to conquer the world. I was free at last, more evolved and living in my light body. I was of the world but had such an incredibly different perspective than the average 'Jen'. Chaos surrounded me, yet I was grounded and sure-footed, each step leading me to my higher self. I felt my aura expand. I had moments of bliss, yet my life was full of uncertainty. Instead of focusing on the challenges of being a single Mom with three kids, recovering from the hell I had been through, I sought opportunity from my gifts.

When I looked in the mirror, I no longer looked for the flaws, the wrinkles and the impending aging. Instead I saw the light in my eyes and I thanked God for restoring my youth each day, for not letting the pain and agony of what I had been through show on my face, for having the ability to heal quickly from each illness and injury. I began to care and be more conscious about what I ate and how I spent my time. I injected this into my children's lives as well. I complimented them more and began to tell Hope how she was growing and becoming slimmer, instead of telling her she needed to watch what she ate. Of course, I interjected with unhealthy choices, but I think she began to buy into my ideas when I was more positive and we played together as a team.

Ten months after Joe passed, I attended a half-day Mediumship Meet Up during March Break. This made the weekend time commitment easier with a week off of school. At the Meet up we brought friends that would be read to by other practicing Mediums. I asked my friend Cassie to join me and she was happy to. We practised psychometry in which we wrote our name on a piece of paper and put it in a basket, then we each picked one name out and without looking at the name, gave a personal message for that person. At the end of our message, we opened the paper up and read the name of the person it was for. I found it easy to get short messages for others, and was told that I was astonishingly accurate.

Next we did four mediumship readings for the guests of other practising Mediums. I gained confidence and experience with these readings and realized I could do it professionally if I chose. In one case, I read the guardian angel of a woman instead of a deceased loved one. I even picked up that she loved sunflowers and that her guardian angel was giving her a symbol each time she meditated on or noticed sunflowers.

During the first round of psychometry, I felt many messages could have been for me from Joe but I was very last and the message from Joe to me was this:

- *The reader was getting red roses (Joe called me his rose and I had just told Cassie how I was thinking about Rose from the movie Titanic when I was walking on the beach in Barbados. When we returned to the room, I turned on the television and this very movie was playing).*
- *The person is a tall, dark haired man standing beside a new vehicle and handing the document to the car, he is a father figure (I just bought a new SUV).*

At the end we practiced psychometry in the same way again. This time the leader of the group Nadine, was first and the message turned out to be for me. She said: "This person works a lot with angels, I'm getting Hawaii, this person should take Doreen Virtue's workshop in Hawaii".

That afternoon I googled to see if this was correct about the workshop. It was correct; Doreen Virtue was coming to Maui on my birthday long weekend in October! Although I would have loved to go, responsibilities at home became more of a priority and I am still wishing for a trip to Hawaii one day.

After the Mediumship Meet up, Hope and I went to the cemetery together to finally pick up the Christmas wreaths on Joe and Joseph's grave before they were discarded by Easter. I felt Joe's presence as I pulled alongside the driveway beside the plot. It was sadly surreal to think I was bringing my nine year old daughter to her father's grave. I sat in the front of our SUV, took a deep breath and sighed. Joe's presence became stronger.

Becoming overwhelmed, I began to cry. I was feeling Joe's emotion and knew he had a message for Hope. I channelled what Joe was saying to her:

You are such a good little girl. I never expected this to happen and I'm sorry. You're such a brave girl! I am so proud of you. You are so strong and smart and I love you!

I also happened to have my James Van Praagh Mediumship Cards in the front seat of the vehicle from earlier that day when I brought them to the mediumship workshop. I pulled a card which said, *"I kiss you goodnight every night."* The card I pulled for me was most appropriate: *"You have nothing to feel guilty for."* The card I pulled for both of us said, *"You are never alone."*

Helping my children through their grief was in many ways more difficult than dealing with my own profound sense of loss. I felt powerless to change the circumstance of losing their father. Nothing I could say or do, could ever take away the hurt they suffered. As strong as my children are, and as much as they understand the spiritual nature of life and death, the unfairness of their father's death in their lives was something I was constantly mediating, at least in my mind.

How I wished Hope and I were not put in that circumstance of visiting her father's grave and me delivering that message from her Dad. I do know, however, that she and her siblings are still blessed to have an incredible guardian angel of a Dad watching over their lives, giving them love, faith and hope that there is so much more to life than what most of us see and experience on this side of the veil.

Chapter 17

On the Stairway to Heaven

"Your greatest awakening comes when you are aware of your infinite nature." ~ Amit Ray

June 2016

Piercing the boundaries of limited thinking became part of my thought process and inspired my fascination with the spiritual realm. Healing for me continued to expand through unconventional means. I refused to limit my concept of self to my physical body, who I knew and what I owned. The emphasis on materialism diminished and I began to become more comfortable with the unknown. All of the expectations for life with Joe were lost and that was something that I was grieving as well. I became more restless trying to live the old life I was living with Joe. Part of me wanted to desperately hang on like a child holds onto a security blanket, but so much of my life was no longer serving me.

A year after Joe's death was a tumultuous time. I was still wrapping up lose ends with his physical death. I was at last coming to terms with the burial arrangement and picking out a headstone for his grave. I was still cleaning up the material mess Joe left and I was anxious to get rid of his less personal belongings such as his tools. I felt entangled by the lose ends he left and was beginning to imagine a life of more material simplicity, owning only what I needed or was especially fond of.

I started to visualize a future where I was true to myself, as I did before I married Joe. Still, I felt caught in a web where old patterns were surfacing with stress, anxiety and relationships. I began to recognize the dysfunction in my relationship with my parents, and at times the conflict magnified itself in very difficult ways. I went through the emotions on a new level with new behaviours. As problems and conflict surfaced, I went through the emotional turmoil with more courage and maturity. Eventually this storm subsided, and the waters calmed. I was at last living more authentically as my true self, on my own terms.

In the end, I gained reverence and respect for my parents as kindred souls on my life path. As difficult as the relationship conflicts were, I hold no anger or hostility towards my family. The circumstances around my husband's death were extraordinary. I was pushed to the limits of a soul experiencing life in a physical body. I have no control over the consciousness and healing of others, but I felt a level of healing deep within me. Forgiveness and grace were the lessons here. When I married Joe, his suicide was the last thing anyone would have expected.

In early June of 2016, I returned to Carol Righton for a Divine Healing Session. She attuned and upgraded my energy to merge even more into the consciousness of unconditional love of divine. With spirit, she worked on my physical body. My communication and channelling with spirit was reduced at that busy time for me. Here is what was said in that session between Carol and I:

Carol: The energy of spirit has been working on our physical body. We are working on the physical body and this could be one of the reasons communications has been slow at this time.

Me: Yes I've noticed that, but I've been really busy. I'm focused more on my body.

Carol: We will also upgrade your beloved's frequency even higher.

Me: Is Joe not at the highest frequency?

Carol: He is, but he's merging even higher. He is in Source, but you're still in a physical body. You're working with the energy and cell memory of mother earth.

Beloved, I Can Show You Heaven

Me: I don't get where he is at. I don't know where he is. I don't know what he is experiencing.

Carol: He feels unconditional love. He sees all, he's in all. The energies are merging to a place where the energies of the planet are of *All* factor, God factor. He's everywhere, he's everywhere where things are still, peaceful and beautiful. He is unconditional love. He's no longer a 'he', he's his higher self in God-consciousness, and he is in his 'I am' consciousness, so you're actually communicating to an aspect of God.

Me: Wow. Is that normal for somebody who has crossed?

Carol: We all merge into our higher selves. Think of it this way (holds hand up), this is his higher self, and his higher self is the God-consciousness of God.

Me: I am not getting things with him as a typical deceased loved one.

Carol: All loved ones are starting to come through that way.

Me: It is like there is no separation.

Carol: What is the separation? It is the earthly body now, that's it. The body lowers the frequency so when you communicate, you're still communicating in a third dimension reality. So when you're going to communicate, you're going to communicate with his old self.

Me: This morning I was changing the station on the satellite radio, and I accidentally flipped to the wrong station and the song was Evanescence, *My Immortal*, and I couldn't tell if the song was communicating from him to me, or if it was me to him, even though it is a female singer. Does that make sense?

Carol: Yeah.

Me: Does he experience pain, or does he miss me?

Carol: He is speaking to you as his higher self. Eventually there will not be a veil to communicate.

Me: I can feel the veil getting thinner between us.

Carol: Eventually there will not be a veil between us and we will all communicate through our higher selves. When you open your vibrational consciousness up, to a fifth, sixth, seventh dimension consciousness, then you're able to communicate in that level. It's when we have emotions like shame, and depression that collapses our fifth dimension matrix.

Me: Um-hmm.

Carol: What you need to understand is your third dimension body is missing him.

Me: Yeah, I kind of only miss him physically.

Carol: That makes sense because you're actually connected to him spiritually. That is why I took you to the energy of the Milky Way. When you get into that energy, you open up and expand.

Me: I cannot even feel anger anymore. I can't even get angry anymore.

Carol: Awesome! That's third dimension energy. That energy collapses the matrix.

Me: I especially cannot feel anger towards him. Sometimes I try and it's just like pshhh....I can't, I can't, its just not there...

Carol: He has been a catalyst of removing that, and you have been a catalyst of merging up where he is, everywhere. Think of it as energy waves, or energy radio waves, that's how you communicate. You're communicating through the vibration of energy.

Me: Right. That's why he is sending me a sign on the radio and I don't know if I just tuned into it or he's sending it to me, or whatever. It could be a little bit of both.

Carol: It's both; he's letting you know that he's there for you.

Me: The only sign I ever get from him lately are chills up my body, up my legs on one side of my body.

Carol: That's good, that's confirmation. So what's he's doing is he's building a connection and you say ah-ha and you start paying attention to the words.

Me: Exactly, he knew I once loved that song, and I once told him the song reminded me of Nicholas because of the words when he was sick.

Carol: It's important to understand that there is a lot of upgrading going on right now. What do I mean by upgrading? There is an expansion in consciousness. Interesting enough, your communication is coming more from your crown now. Do you feel it?

Me: Yup.

Carol: So that means it's really angelically, divinely being channelled to you. There is a difference; with soul guides you will feel the energy at your sides. When it comes straight through the consciousness of God and the Archangels, it comes through the crown. When I was setting the fifth dimension chakras, I felt the information that you're now channelling is coming from your crown, which means that you are working with the heart angel. It means you are working with the angel that works with the understanding of unconditional love. How does that feel?

Me: It feels like its coming from the top of my head. I cannot get my attention off the top of my head.

Carol: A baby is born with a soft crown at the top of the head. That is the vortex that connects exactly with the pineal gland. Your being angelically, wait…Is it angelic? It's interesting because your ability to channel is past the angelic realm now. So we opened your galactic star. Well who watches over the galactic star but Metatron. It's interesting how Metatron came through to put his cube in your chakra system.

Me: Oh, okay, so it's not the same for everyone?

Carol: Haven't done that for anyone.

Me: I think he's coming through to Faith. She's writing a story that is very mathematical how everybody dies. She's really getting stuff.

Carol: That's awesome.

Me: I can channel Source. On the one year anniversary of Joe's death, I meditated and went directly to Source. I asked God if it was my fault that Joe died. And God said to me as I bathed in his beautiful light two questions: One, "Did you intend for it to happen, did you want for it to happen?" (Of course not) And the other question he asked me was, "Did you do anything to cause this to happen?" I said "No, I did what I could to stop it."

It doesn't matter that some told me that I should not feel guilty, this was the thing that put it to rest. On the other side of Source there was Joe with a child beside him. I believe it was Joseph.

Carol: That's perfect! You went right into Source. So the way that I am finding that people can go to Source is through the Milky Way energy.

Me: I feel like I can go straight there.

Carol: I have to tell you that you need your soul guides. We come in with the consciousness of a body and we come with the consciousness of Source. We're also all cells of the mother earth. So whatever has happened on Mother Earth is imprinted in all cells of the body.

The third dimension body goes back to Earth when a person dies. So when I'm reading the deceased they will say I passed from this, this, and this. Once that connection is made, they go back into their light body, their higher self. I do not want to connect to the energy of mother earth but to the infinite intelligence of her, her God Source. Her God Source is very wise, very healing to my body, so I always connect to the infinite intelligence of Mother Earth for the highest and best of all involved.

Me: Interesting, I've been more protective of her at work, like with the kids. I say, 'Leave the insects outside, they don't go to school, you go to school.' Or I've been gardening and that is not like me.

Carol: The reason Mother Earth is communicating with you is because she knows you write, so she wants to communicate with you. She is calling you in because she knows you will have a voice for her, and you teach, so that's Mother Gaia. The soul is electromagnetic, the Earth is magnetic. They merged together and created.

Me: It's like with kids. If I ask, 'Where is your soul?' They point to their heart. We're drawn to love from our heart.

Carol: It's also interesting because the heart actually has brain cells. The soul guides are there because we come in with energy which is unique to you. You have that protection that is a combination of Mother Earth and that cell memory and Source. We are both in a physical body. Our guides are both in spirit, as they were once in a physical body.

Me: What's interesting about the Meditation that took place on May 13, 2016, is that when I went to Source, Joe was standing by with the energy of my son, as a guide would. I felt him and our son there, standing by my side with soul guide energy, non-interfering, but present. When I was bathed in the light of God Source, I knew I was not alone, but Joe and our son did not interfere in any way with my connection and communication with Source. I felt their presence and in some ways they made the experience more tangible as they held space for me at Source.

Chapter 18

Messages from My Beloved

*"The soulmate relationship goes beyond 'Til death do us part':
for true love never dies." - Richard Webster*

Mediumship Workshop – June 2016

I finally enrolled in a weekend long Mediumship Course. I wanted to gain confidence in my abilities as a medium. I wondered if I was really good enough to give professional readings to others from their deceased loved ones. However, my strongest motivation was to develop my skills to connect better with my beloved husband. Receiving a weekend of healing messages from like minded spiritualists was the icing on the cake.

I remember the beginning of the workshop on Friday evening. The teacher Chris gave us minutes of silence to take a pad and a paper and write down the names of all the deceased loved ones we were getting. I think my list was the longest as they seemed to come easily to me, one after another. Chris asked me to read the names on my list and I was astonished at how the other participants recognized these names as their own deceased loved ones, even the highly unusual name 'Maverick' was the name of one ladies deceased ex-husband.

It was a beautiful, sunny weekend in early summer at the lake house where the workshop was held on the shores of the lake. The sun glistened in the large bright window of the angelic room at the back of the house. There was comfort and peace, like the gentle brush of angel wings.

Between the theory that was taught to us, were opportunities for practicing with a different partner, and taking turns each time. Whether I was first or second of each practice, it was as though each mini-reading for me contained a sacred message from Joe which scaffolded to the most profound, healing reading at the end of the weekend. I feel that Joe carefully choose his Medium for each message and the way each message was presented.

Clearly I was meant to be there, although my healing journey was full of ebbs and flows like the waves on the shore, sometimes turbulent and sometimes gentle, I was feeling the calmness in my soul, and this weekend was a period of growth and heavenly peace, even if only for a short time.

The first reading was from Michelle, a bubbly woman about my age with an exuberant personality and a youthful glow. Here is what Michelle said:

"I am seeing a golden light with this person. He's showing you cleaning the house. He was a very quiet person. He's telling me he sees things more positively now; he sees more joy. He's showing me glasses, to show how things are clearer for him now...He's showing you gratitude and has all over joy. I see this amazing blue light around his heart; he is pouring love on you. He is very determined to play a role for you; he wants you to find peace."

"He's so visual; he's showing me a green ball of energy now with a yellow tone. There is such vivid imagery. He's showing me a boat on the water, you are in the boat, and oh, there is a reflection when you look into the water, but you see him when you look down, he is your reflection!"

A funny thing happened during this reading: We were sitting beside the large living room window and just outside the window there was a groundhog that came out of the bush as if it was Joe patiently waiting for the reading to begin and giving me a sign that he is there. I looked up the symbolism of groundhog and this is what it said: "Lessons associated with death, dying and revelations about its processes will begin to surface; how to go into the unconscious without harm. This is often the totem of mystics and shamans."

In the following practice, I telepathically asked our late son Joseph to come through. Coincidentally in the following practice reading, there were two groundhogs, one young and one old. To me it seemed like they were coming out as a father and son and the young one was very active and excited as the parent waited, looking up at us in anticipation.

Roz was my partner, and she read the males in spirit:

"I am getting 2 males, one young and one old. The young one has dark hair with a wave of light brown hair. His hair has lots of body and he has brown eyes. He is about five foot nine inches tall. This younger male is above you, watching you like an angel. He says, *'That's my girl!'* He's very proud of you."

"The older one is with him. I am seeing the word L-O-V-E in big bold letters behind you, they're spelling out how much they love you!"

My next message was from Madelyn. She described a man in his forties that died too young. She said, "He's affirming to you how well you have taken care of everything and he is seeking forgiveness."

He's calling you "Boo"

"That's what he used to call me when we started dating!"

"He's happy about how things are going with the child who plays soccer."

"That's Hope."

"I see you in a small white speedboat. He's saying he's sorry he did not affirm how capable and good you are at things. He wishes he had expressed this to you. He wants you to buy the boat. He says you can manage it by yourself."

While driving back to the workshop on the Sunday morning, one of Joe's favourite old songs from high school was on the radio. It was Depeche Mode, *Enjoy the Silence.* It reminded me of Joe in such a strong way and gave me comfort with the words: *"All I ever wanted, all I ever needed is here in my arms, Words are so very unnecessary, they can only do harm."*

Joe was a very visual and creative person. Unlike me, he didn't use words to express himself, and in hindsight I wish I could have had a view to the visions in his mind. Although many of us are like Joe, what I have learned is the importance of words in expressing gratitude and love to those closest to us. Although I am aware of how much I meant to Joe, there were times when I needed to hear it. From Joe's perspective on the other side, I know he wishes he had been more expressive about what I meant to him.

But we're all different. Some of us are visual, some of us auditory, some of us are cognizant and intellectual, and others are especially sensitive to the vibes and feelings we get from others. This carries over with us when we die. For example, a deceased loved one who used to talk a lot will still talk a lot when coming through in a mediumship reading. My grandmother is one such example; she always had a lot to say. Joe was very visual, and likes to give colours and symbols and pictures to mediums. My son Joseph always carries a peaceful, angelic feeling.

The same is true for Mediums, for example, some Mediums are auditory, or clairaudient and have clear hearing. Clairvoyants see pictures; clairsentients have clear feelings and claircognizants just know things. My strongest clairs may be claircognizance (clear knowing) and clairaudience (clear hearing). During a reading I may pick up on the sense of communication that was strongest for the deceased loved one.

The last and most profound reading of the workshop that Sunday afternoon was during the Group Reading practice. The message was delivered by Sarah, a mother of four children. Sarah had a soft feminine demeanour about her with her long light brown hair and her big light brown eyes. She described a male who was with me.

Sarah saw the male in a garage looking through bins with tools, nuts, and bolts and locks (my garage was still full of tools and Joe even had owned several padlocks). She said it is so overwhelming that she felt dizzy. She said this person was very detached in life but he loves me very much. He didn't verbalize that, but he felt it strongly. Although soft-spoken, Sarah continued with conviction:

"There was no verbal communication. He very much respects you. He tells you that you are capable of doing this. He says to hold strong space for the children. He says to be confident. Your daughter needs that from you! She is fragile inside. Your daughter Hope is more fragile inside, its inside that she is more affected, you may not see."

"I see the girls in the water. It makes him happy. He is with them. He says to let them know that he is around them all the time. Even on their wedding day – he will make sure they make the right choice of man, but they will look to your behaviour."

"Allow yourself space to grow. Forgive yourself. He says *none of this is your fault!* He's using the tools as a metaphor. He's saying get rid of them, get rid of the weight!"

Then Sarah took a deep breath and with all the conviction from Joe said, "YOU ARE AMAZING!!! YOU CAN DO THIS!!! HE LOVES YOU!!!"

When she was done, everyone in the group was in awe and amazement. The power of this soft spoken woman's message from my husband on the other side was visibly moving in this group reading to everybody in the room. Those words of love and conviction remained in my heart for months to know that I am loved, and to give me the confidence in myself as a highly capable woman and mother who is capable of amazing things.

When it was all over and we said our goodbyes, I drove down the beautiful tree-lined street and turned on the radio. The song was *The Time of My Life,* the last song from the movie *Dirty Dancing.* This song was perfectly fitting and gave me amazing closure on Joe's life. It was if he was saying what a wonderful life he had with me:

Now I've had the time of my life
No I've never felt this way before
Yes I swear it's the truth and I owe it all to you
And I've searched through every door
Till I found the truth
And I owe it all to you…

Chapter 19

When Tomorrow Starts Without You

"A raindrop on your cheek is a kiss from someone that lives in Heaven and is watching over you." - behappyzone.com

The summer of 2016 was another difficult one as I was dealing with the physical consequences of my loss. My physical self begged for attention and I needed to heal many aspects of myself including the emotional, and psychological. I was now much more realistic about my physical limitations, while paradoxically recognizing myself as a limitless divine being of God. Fortunately, I had done the inner work that would no longer allow myself to plunge my soul into the depths of despair I was in the summer before.

Although I was struggling a great deal physically, I was aware of how I was evolving as a soul. I came to the realization with my doctor that I needed more time to heal my body in my bereavement and so I took time off of work. I had taken lessons from my past and from the tragic ending of Joe not seeking respite on the physical plane. I had to be wise and take care of myself, for if I could not do it for me, no one else would. I needed to be stronger than ever for my kids, and reconstruct my inner world for our survival.

Reiki had been another catalyst in healing my spirit. I became a Certified Reiki Practitioner and each course provided incredible healing for me and gave me comfort in the presence of healing spirits on my journey. Each attunement ascended the frequency of my vibration even higher. It was taking my first Reiki workshop in the summer of 2015, just two months after Joe died that gave me an incredible tool that literally allowed me to get myself out of a major depressed state by using the first Reiki symbol (Cho Ku Rei) on my body to lift my energy so I could get out of bed and function.

In Reiki One, I was on the table receiving Reiki when the Master and the other students felt the presence of my husband around my aura. The Master softly guided Joe and told him to 'go to the light.' In this sense, Reiki improved my energy because Joe ascended higher on the other side. At the time, part of me didn't want to let go but now I understand that this did not mean that he was leaving me, but that he was still with me in a higher energetic frequency. This was healthier for me.

In Reiki Three, I vividly remember the attunement with my Reiki Master Teacher. During the attunement meditation, I walked with an Amazon Spirit Guide to an Amazon Rainforest hut and waited for the Shaman. As I laid on the ground of the hut, and the Master came around in the attunement, I had a vision of my body shaking and trembling out all pain and negativity in my heart chakra.

When we were practicing healings on each other, I heard in the distance beautiful Reiki music that I thought was coming from the stereo behind the table. One of the other students said, "Does anyone else hear that music?" because in actual fact it was coming from the spirits of our Reiki guides, and we all heard it. I was astonished to have heard something so clearly with my ears and its source, purely spiritual.

I wanted to continue with the healing benefits of Reiki and therefore Karuna Reiki really spoke to me in terms of its benefits of loving compassion and healing the mind's energy. In that class, just as I was beginning to doubt and question the power of Reiki and starting to feel like it was a bit 'woo-hoo', and all in my mind, I was overtaken during the chanting session when we were sitting in a circle in a small room chanting. I actually began to smell a campfire. My eyes started to dart around the enclosed space, and I checked and reminded myself that the Teacher did not light anything before we began. Then the man in our group, sitting beside me stated that he could smell the fire that had been created on the floor between us. I felt relieved both because I had an explanation for what my senses were telling me, and second because I was given awesome confirmation in the truth and power of Reiki, once again in my doubting moment.

I had come so far in only a year, despite the fact that my healing journey of bereavement was far from over. It was during the Karuna Reiki attunement that I also realized how far Joe had come as well. Especially in terms of the role he played for me. Joe was no longer a lingering spirit around my aura who was full of regret and remorse for having ended his life. He had ascended from his lower self to his fully awakened higher self.

In the Attunement Meditation, our Master did a guided meditation which led us down a beautiful path to a beautiful room to meet all of our soul guides. In the beautiful room, one of our soul guides came to meet us and give us a message. Joe was the first guide I met, dressed in a white button up shirt and tan slacks. All the other guides were blurry, faceless forms of spirits, but Joe held me on a sofa in the large, family room with a wall of glass windows. I sat on his lap like a child and he held me protectively as he soothed me lovingly with his words. I felt like a baby who had just fallen asleep in her protective father's arms and the father did not want the baby disturbed. Joe told me how much he loved me and held my pain. He said that there was nothing I needed to know as I sat there with tears pouring down my cheeks. He held my head and whispered in my ears, and though I forget all he said, I remember the way I felt the peace and love and the comfort in receiving from him the highest and the best from the only one who could make me feel so special. My beloved possessed God's eternal love and it brings me comfort that heaven is a place of love where my beloved is with me as a guardian and guide.

About six months after Joe died I investigated Joe's complaints about work before he died. During this investigation, I became briefly acquainted with the man who was helping me. He asked me to coffee a couple of times and I did not know what to make of it and did not give it much thought in my busy life. The following September, he re-introduced himself into my life when an opportunity presented itself. At the time, I wondered if there could ever be someone else that I had an attraction and feelings for and he seemed to appear out of thin air.

His entry was jarring. I had just started to focus on my needs when he declared his attraction for me. Before that, I truthfully was unsure where our connection stood, and if he was just a kind, hard-working employee.

Though I had come so far on my own, I knew I was not yet ready for a relationship. During this time I received a great deal of guidance from Joe with respect to him. I believe I was meant to have the experience to teach me I was capable of having feelings for someone else. At the same time I learned that I am an attractive woman with a lot of life left in me. I know he was attracted to my energy, and perhaps since he is older, I made him feel young again.

In entering the world of dating, Joe was fully there to give me messages to guide me and my beliefs in myself. I wasn't ready for a relationship and came to the ultimate conclusion through total discouragement that there would not be anyone suitable for me until I had come into a relationship with myself. My confidence was diminished from a seemingly failed monogamous relationship of two and a half decades. I learned that I was not only attractive to Joe, but to other men as well. Unfortunately, to me, no one compared to Joe in any way. It seemed what we shared was too special to experience again in a new and different way. I wondered still if we only get one true soul mate relationship. I really just wanted Joe and my old life back, but in Joe's death, he reassured me of my worth and value to another partner. Joe insisted I not settle, and at times played the protector from those he knew were unsuitable.

There were three poignant examples of these messages coming through three different mediums, one of which was a Medium named Catherine MacDonald, who I contacted at the end of September 2016. The other was through an unexpected source, an exterminator from a pest control company that came to give me a quote when I thought I had mice in my attic. The third was through my friend Greg who Joe also contacted one evening after over a year of not having interaction with.

On occasional nights throughout the summer of 2016, I heard rustling in the ceiling over my bedroom. I had a racoon problem the previous February and had spent $1300 racoon proofing my roof and so I thought the sounds I was hearing was the wind in the master bedroom washroom vent. One night in September it was particularly bad and I couldn't sleep any longer in the early hours of the morning. I immediately got on the phone, looking for a solution. After a few calls, I found a company who felt I had a mouse problem and was willing to come out at the end of that Friday afternoon to give me a free quote. In desperation, I took their last appointment of the day.

When the man came to give me the quote, I answered the door anxiously and he joked with me about two large daddy-long leg spiders that were at the top of my front door on either side. He was a shorter man with a shaved head, medium build wearing baggy workman like clothes, smelling of strong cologne. In a jovial and surprised tone, he asked me, "What's with the two spiders you have here?" I looked out my door and up at them, and as if I knew they were there all along. I quickly replied, "They are my guardians. Some people have lions, but these guys are my guards, protecting my house." We chuckled and I met him in my backyard. Although I didn't say it, I thought to myself that it was a sign from Joe, and mused at his sense of humour, as this reminded me of the clever things Joe would do in life.

The pest control person's name was Alex and he seemed to like me instantly but I was apprehensive about him. I told him I was a single Mom and widow only because I thought it might give me a better price on the estimate. He was very sympathetic to my loss but I told him I really didn't want to talk about it. When I told him I had a nineteen year old son, he was surprised and flattered me by saying that I didn't even look old enough to have children. He told me I had amazing eyes and smile and by then I thought for sure this guy was hitting on me. I laughed at the uncomfortable flattery and Alex started to ask me what I did for fun, "I like you Jen, you're really cool. What do you like to do for fun?"

I told him I am intuitive and did Reiki and stuff and he was surprised and told me he did the same.

He said something which led me to remember something in our home that was coming from the fruit cellar ceiling and I wanted him to check if it was coming from insects or mice. I was getting a headache from his cologne and apprehensive about it getting worse with him being in my home. I came right out and honestly told him that I was very sensitive to scent and he was very cool about it. He laughed at my honesty.

We went downstairs and he was really impressed with my finished basement in addition to the rest of the house. He told me, "Jen, you are the perfect woman in every way. You are so smart, any guy would be so lucky to have you." Again I laughed to ease my discomfort and when he was checking out Joe's old shop, the fruit cellar, he kept talking to me. As I stood outside the room, he told me I am funny and he hopes I have fun sometimes. I began to feel very sad and tried not to cry. That room was difficult for me to be in, and I was releasing the stress that had been accumulating for days, especially thinking I had huge mice problems. I also had major pool issues and had just had a hole in my pool liner repaired.

Alex felt terrible I was crying and before we went back upstairs, he asked me if I had any water for him. I instantly passed him a bottle of water from my basement refrigerator and joked with him that at the speed I had manifested the water, it was magic. This led to a brief discussion on quantum physics and I walked up the stairs behind him. At the top of the stairs there was water on the floor which I noticed when I stepped in it. I sarcastically made a comment to Alex about the mess he had made on my floor as I grabbed paper towels from the kitchen to wipe it up.

Alex laughed and as he sat at my table, he began to tell me exuberantly things he knew about life and love. He told me how things are not the same when you get older, not to find an older man because that would not make me happy. I continued to laugh at his advice and he continued to question me, and what I like to do on dates. I hadn't really dated anyone except my husband and I uncomfortably began to feel that he was going to ask me out but he told me he had a girlfriend. The advice about older men struck me as quite a coincidence as I had not told him about the older man I had a romantic encounter with.

I showed him my first book and he was very impressed, continuing on with praising me and after knowing he was committed to his girlfriend, I began to relax and sat down across from him to talk. He began to tell me how I needed someone that, "Is going to treat me like the queen you are. You are majestic!"

The flattery was so rich, all about my intelligence, my looks and especially my level of spirit. He held his hands up, "You are here, and all the other guys are in third dimension, down here. You need someone who is going to treat you like the queen you are, up here."

"Wow," I said as he went on. It was becoming as if Alex's face was shape shifting and I was no longer seeing him but hearing Joe's nature of complimenting me. Nobody had complimented me or felt that way about me before, except Joe.

The conversation turned back to Joe as Alex noticed across the family room, a picture of Joe on the fireplace mantle. I brought it over to him and

Alex looked at Joe with humility saying, "What a great guy. He's a nice guy, a very nice guy. But something's missing. I feel it in his eyes. I see depression, especially at the end, but he didn't want to burden you guys with it."

Alex continued, "I have a confession to make: When I was downstairs in the workshop, I felt someone push the back of my knee and I lost my balance. When I was walking up the stairs, I heard low voices whispering and your husband asked me to stay awhile and talk to you. I never do that. This is just between you and me, don't tell my company this."

I told him how I felt it was as if what he was saying was my husband was speaking to me, not him. Alex confessed that was how he felt also. I felt deep gratitude to this stranger that gave me wonderful messages of love to remind me of how special I am and the kind of relationship I deserve. Alex left saying that his company would call me tomorrow with their price, and the next day, their handyman gave me a quote for over $2000 to seal all the holes in my home exterior. I was floored at the cost, but somehow, that sound did not come back and I never had mice in my home. I did receive however, a beautiful message from my beloved at the time I really needed it.

Joe continued to guide me from the other side and I experienced the misfortune of having difficulty with our pool. This frustration led me to book a reading with Catherine MacDonald, a Psychic-Medium I had not spoken to in over five years. Somehow I felt that Catherine was the right person to speak with at this time. Her style proved to be what I needed to hear from Joe at this time about sixteen months after his death. Here is the reading with Catherine MacDonald:

Catherine: I am getting a male around you who you are trying to contact. I feel like a family member, but I am not sure if it is your family or Joe's family. I think its Joe's family.

Me: Do you remember Joe?

Catherine: Yes, I remember him briefly; he's quite a tall fella. I think it's his Dad that's around, a man with a leather coat.

Me: Can you give me one more piece of information about the man?

Catherine: The man is someone we've read before, someone close to you. He comes forward.

Me: It's Joe. Joe died. Did you get that?

Catherine: Joe died? (Long pause). Joe died? Oh my goodness, he's very much like the man I've read for!

Me: It is Joe, he died May 2015.

Catherine: Ooh my goodness, I'm sorry. I just keep getting the guy with the leather coat.

Me: It's definitely Joe.

Catherine: Oh my goodness, I feel like it wasn't supposed to happen, or very sudden, like a shock. Did he have something with the heart Hun, breathing, chest, whatever. I keep getting anxiety.
   I see very tall, dark hair, grey in it, but mostly dark hair, longish? He could be quite intimidating if he wanted to but he's a big teddy bear. He was a sweetheart when it came to working with you guys.
   Sudden, really sudden, I keep getting pain around the chest.

Me: You know what; let's just talk to him because he took his life.

Catherine: Oh my goodness honey, he wasn't bringing it that way though, unless he's talking about heartaches.

Me: Yes, exactly, I am intuitive too, I have no question about what you do or if it's him. I have questions for him, so I just want to cut to the chase.

Catherine: Okay, it didn't feel like a heart attack, it just felt like heavy hearted. Oh my goodness, it wasn't supposed to happen. He didn't expect to be successful. He felt like a failure in a whole bunch of other areas, which he was not, but he realized that he made that mistake. However, he is there and his grandfather is with him. I hear 'Dad.'

Beloved, I Can Show You Heaven

Me: That could be our son.

Catherine: Okay, they are coming very quickly. What do you want to know?

Me: I want to know about romantic relationships and where my life is headed in that direction.

Catherine: Okay, he's coming across as very protective of you. If you're dealing with someone right now, you're not really ready, but it's fine to get on with life. Now I understand what the chaos has been about. You're shell shocked because you never thought he would do something like that.

Me: Going back to his death though, from a soul point of view, was this in our contract and supposed to happen?

Catherine: This is one of his exit points, yes, it was still a choice, but it does fulfil his soul contract, and he could have waited and gone on in another time, and another way. There is something about feeling very burdened and overwhelmed all the time. I never got that impression from him when I met him. Was he really good at hiding it?

Me: He was really good at hiding it and he also did a nosedive because of the situation at work, things were kind of getting better in terms of my son's health. He was working night shift and he was exhausted!

Catherine: It does fulfil his soul contract; he wasn't supposed to be here for a long time. He got you to a better place where your son is in a better place. He felt like he caused most of the problems in your life together and he took the blame for it, and he shouldn't have.

I keep hearing the word harassment. There was harassment happening, he was really having a tough time on the night shift and he was feeling harassed or harangued by the amount of work. The load of work was getting to him, and he didn't know how to say 'no', and that was his mistake. He was trying to be all things to everybody.

He is not going to be punished for this. He already went through his hell. He did have depression, but he usually managed really well. The night shift was not good for his body. He was not able to sleep during the day. So he says it was part of his soul contract to exit earlier. He's one of those guys that are there for a good time, but not a long time. He always had the sense that he wouldn't be around for a long time. I don't know if he ever told you that.

Me: Yeah, once I said to him, 'Take care of yourself, I want to be with you until our 90's', but he didn't respond to my point.

Catherine: He didn't have the self-esteem to do that honey. He always thought that you were too good for him, he loved you, but he didn't think he could take care of you the way that you deserved and the burden and the heavy-heartedness got to him. He realizes now that's wrong thinking. He says he makes a better kick-ass guardian angel, you've got him and his grandfather and your son…

Your son keeps saying 'Dad'. To me, it's like a teenager saying, 'but Dad', and I'm going to ask him to stop doing that because he's messing me up. I feel like a grandfather with him, you've got the whole family on your side. Okay? He keeps wanting to apologize to you for letting you down.

Me: Mm-hum.

Catherine: He didn't realize how sick he was. The sleep deprivation was making him nutty. He thought he could handle it, does that make sense?

With the grandfather, I'm getting like a beige, dress-leather coat. With Joe I am getting a biker leather coat, it's black. It's a nice looking jacket, he's showing me it. Did he have a leather coat?

Me: Maybe he always wanted one, he does have one that's not a biker jacket but its black and short leather.

Catherine: To me, that kind of thing is about protection. He's trying to be tougher than he was, and he's really a big softy, he really was, and he didn't know how to ask for help.

This is not your fault, you tried to give him good advice, you tried to get him to do what he needed to do, and he was too stubborn.

You now have your son with you, the one that is alive. Does he have dreams and nightmares?

Me: He used to have nightmares. He's told me about recent good dreams lately.

Catherine: He's fine now; Joe and your son have worked something out. Your daughters, not as much, they don't communicate with him as much. It doesn't bother them in the same way. Your son is super sensitive like his Dad. Okay? And the girls are more like you, tough as nails, and they sense and see things but that's normal.

Me: And they talk about it, and they're open about it.

Catherine: Yeah, they find it easier to talk about so it's not as scary. Okay, so that is where you are with the kids, and you're doing the right things. He's very pleased. You have questions for him?

Me: My question is: My first kind of 'romantic relationship' recently started. It was someone I met because of the circumstances around Joe's death. He occasionally e-mailed or texted me, and I didn't know what to make of it.

Catherine: He's not a bad guy, Joe doesn't dislike him. You're not ready.

Me: He told me his feelings. He's older. That makes me uneasy and I'm afraid of losing someone again. I can't go through that and take that risk.

Catherine: Joe says he's always liked the guy but he's saying trust your gut. Your not willing to take all that on. I feel like he is attracted to you. He really likes you, he likes your energy; you make him feel young. He's not a bad guy. There is some real connection between the two of you. I'm not sure if it is much on your side as his side, but he feels very drawn to you. I don't think he can make the changes in his life that will lead you two to a full-time relationship. Like Joe says, 'You're not ready and this isn't the guy.' Joe didn't want to interfere also because he wanted you to trust your own gut, but he's saying you already know that this isn't what you want.

Me: Yeah, it's confusing.

Catherine: He's trying to give you the benefit of the doubt and saying, this would not be good for you because there is chaos with it. You've had enough chaos.

Me: I have.

Catherine: Tell him that you need real stability in your life and you need time alone. Joe says this is a really bad idea for you, because you will get attached to him. He's not mad at you, he says 'I left you in a really raw place, and I did something really stupid, and I left you high and dry', and that is the way he's putting it. I have a feeling you won't talk to him until next week because of the chaos in his life. He's going to keep doing that, and you're going to say 'I can't do this anymore'. You will be the – uh, break-up person. It's easier for you to do that. And you didn't screw it up. He wanted you and he went for it, a little selfish on his part, but it was flattering for you, and you trusted him and felt safe with him. He's been a good guy in other ways. We're all complicated people; nobody is all good or all bad. We're all grey.

Me: What about other relationships? Is there somebody else that is part of my life contract?

Catherine: I feel there will be someone, it feels like a good fit, he makes you laugh, the conversations are easy, the texting is fun. That is a person who is a really good relationship for you. It is another person that you could have a really intense connected soul mate relationship with. I think you and this person will be on the same wavelength.

Me: Is this guy part of my contract?

Catherine: These are all lessons. That other guy was about you having to set the standard in your life and learning that saying 'no' is not fatal. For you, he is a lesson in that you are still attractive, you are still a very, very vivacious person that people are still interested in. You will decide that you don't want that kind of drama.

Me: So when Joe exited, was a new person contracted to come into my life?

Catherine: Yes, so that you could have another loving relationship. You're not meant to be alone for years and years. If you decide you're not ready, and you want to be alone for longer, it just delays the contract.

Me: So the choices are about the time, but it's ultimately meant to be my destiny?

Catherine: Yes, well Joe made his choice and now the universe needs to work with what is been given. Joe made his choice at one of his exit points in his contract. If he hadn't exit-pointed then, he probably would have exit-pointed in a few more years. That is what he's saying, so now they are bringing someone good for you, that will *be* someone that you can count on, and someone that is stable. Because even though Joe had all those issues, he loved you dearly, and you will have that again. He's not like Joe, but you will feel blessed.

It may take time for that happen, because you may decide to wait because you really loved Joe. It's one of those major life relationships.

Me: We were together 25 years.

Catherine: Wow. You were together longer than most people are married now.

He's not offended by you finding someone new, because you're young. There is quite an age difference between the two of you, correct?

Me: Joe and I? No. We were in the same grade; less than 2 years.

Catherine: He always thought of himself as an old man and you were too young for him, I don't know why.

Me: He always said I was like a teenager, I was 18 when we started going out.

Catherine: He says that you have lots of love and life left. He always thought of himself as an old man, and as holding you back, which is not true! He realizes that was an error in his thinking, but he says he loves you and you will find somebody, and he will help you. That dude is not it. There is always the weird space in the in-between. You're confused right now and that weird energy is drawing in a confused person. And your own gut is telling you that, so Joe is giving you space with that.

Me: So if Joe didn't die now, he would die in a few years?

Catherine: Yeah in the next three to five years, or early fifties or something like that. Something else would have occurred; it didn't have to be a suicide. You had said you wanted him to be here a long time and he couldn't answer you.

Me: Yes, he just told me I am the sweetest thing in the world.

Catherine: Yes, he just had this feeling he wasn't supposed to be here for a long time, and he didn't want to say that and ruin the moment. He wasn't supposed to be here a long time, I'm not sure why, but now that he's your Guardian Angel, he feels like he can do better for you.

Me: Yeah, I've started writing, and he's a guide.

Catherine: He says he can do better on the spirit side for you than he ever could in life.

Me: Although he did well in life, but I know what he's saying. Can I ask you about the pool? There are issues that keep coming up.

Catherine: He likes to mess with the equipment.

Me: Why the hell would he do that?

Catherine: So you would phone about the reading. It's kind of his way of letting you know he's there. He's also letting you know to pay attention to your pool, and to close it and deal with it in the spring. He's saying 'Call the damn pool company and get them to come here and fix it!' *Ha! ha! ha!*

You know that the guy loves you and he always has, he just never thought that he was good enough for you, and that is what all of this nonsense is about, and the heavy heart stuff and I don't think he ever told you but I don't think he ever got over the loss of your son.

Me: Yeah, I had that sense too.

Catherine: He never told you or made an issue out of it. He felt it was his fault and he took the blame for it.

Me: Was that my fault? Like I said something in a heated fight?

Catherine: No I don't think so; he's the type of guy that would have taken the blame anyway. He understood that was the most emotional thing you have ever gone through, and he loves you and he doesn't hold onto that now. He understands that you were both dealing with the grief. He understands that you needed to talk about it, but he couldn't talk about that, and you needed to.

Me: My son is having a hard time doing things around the house.

Catherine: He wasn't ready to be the man of the house. He will come to his own; it's been a rough 16 months.

Me: Is he okay in school?

Catherine: Oh yeah, he's kind of coasting, not working to his full-potential. He's a bright kid, but he's just sort of getting over things. And he blames himself, and I don't know if they had some kind of disagreement or words, and Nicholas is blaming himself.

Me: Yes, there were things Joe said to him because I was upset with Nicholas.

Catherine: Joe says, 'Tell him it's not that. Its things that were very personal to Dad, things that you know as Mom, with work and the burn out and the lack of sleep, and he had dealt with depression in the past. It wasn't that one thing that pushed him over the edge.

He's taking the blame for it and that is the one thing that Joe is really hurt about. He didn't stop and think who he was going to hurt and how. He just wanted to stop the pain and the frustration and the feeling of overwhelm. He wasn't thinking about who it was going to hurt.

Me: With his work, the claim was unsuccessful without documentation…

Catherine: And he didn't do things right and he knew it was going to be costly and expensive, and there was worry about that, and he was thinking it might be easier if he did what he did. I don't know, his thinking was all messed up.

Was he on pain medication? His thinking was all messed up like he had been taking something for pain.

Me: No, but he might have been in pain, unless he was taking something without my knowing. He was a martyr, and he wouldn't take medication if he needed it.

Catherine: Because I have chronic pain and sometimes pain makes you do nutty things. That's where I'm going with it because he keeps saying 'I have pain, I just wanted to stop the pain.'

Me: I know I have pain too.

Catherine: I don't think he ever thought he would be successful. He just wanted the ride to stop, he wanted to get off. I think he just wanted to stop the pain and the chaos. He's not even showing how he did it.

Me: He hung himself.

Catherine: Oh my goodness, that's why the chest, if he choked me I wouldn't be able to talk. I didn't make the connection. He just wanted you to know to tell Nicholas that it is not his fault. Does Nicholas believe in this stuff?

Me: Oh yes, I can do mediumship so this is normal.

Catherine: Just tell him none of this is his fault. Joe was in his own pain, and his judgement was right off from the lack of sleep and the pain.

Me: Did he have a demon?

Catherine. No, no. That may be the way he described what was going on in his head but no he didn't have anything negative around him in that sense. He did see and sense things but they were not connected to him. He thought they might be.

Me: Like, what did he see?

Catherine: I think he was aware of people's negative potential. He would pick up on that stuff. Some people see things as elementals.

Me: He would identify with colours, he would say 'They are very dark' or to me, he'd say, 'You're such a light'. He would describe people as very grey and he was leery.

Catherine: So he's seeing them as grey, dark, black, light, white, gotcha.

He might have thought there was something negative around him because his mood was negative, but I'm not getting that there was something that made him do this. I'm getting that he was very affected by the energies that were around him.

What you focus on is what you see, right? What he is saying is because his thinking was all 'f**ked up', his words, not mine, you know me, I'm careful about swearing… he's laughing. He's saying his thinking was so f**ked up that he wouldn't be able to properly figure out who was around. There are energies that will mess with your head if you're in a low enough space. I've been there and deal with depression. He was very overwhelmed by what's going on in the world too. He was very aware and worried for the next generation, it was almost too much to handle.

Me: Yeah, and he wasn't brought up equipped for that.

Catherine: No, he was a rough guy, and his family brought him up not to talk about certain things. They were a good family, they just weren't emotionally caddy. They didn't have that repertoire, that language.

Me: Can I ask you a question? When Hope was three she was very psychic and used to talk about heaven. She used to talk about her other brother and sister and other Dad. I would say, 'Is there another mom?' and she would say, 'No there is just you, Mom.' When I was pregnant with her I had a couple of dreams that were distressing because in the dream, Joe was not her father. When he was young, did his soul split? Was he not all there in spirit?

Catherine: Well he might have been one of these guys that really didn't feel like he belonged here. He had that connection to spirit but he didn't know how to handle it, that's why when he was younger he would drink, not a lot. So with your daughter she was just aware of Daddy's other side, because there was this rough and hard working guy and she could see through all of that and was aware of the other side of him that was very spiritual.

Me: Funny, I used to have dreams years ago when the kids were very small that there were two Joe's, one in heaven I could not get close to, but every time I got close, he had to go, and then there was my husband who is a regular guy who was rough around the edges.

Catherine: He was very connected to the spirit realm and didn't know how to handle that. That's the feeling that I get. There was a feeling that your daughter didn't really know how to interpret what the message was.

Me: Thank you very much, that's very insightful.

Catherine: Yes we've gone over but it's my early Christmas present to you. He asked me to do you that favour because there are a lot of adjustments and funds are tight.

Me: Thank you, I'm sure the universe will pay you back.

Catherine: He says your daughter still has her dreams. Your son, he says, is overwhelmed, and he didn't expect to be the man of the house at such a young age. Your husband was very protective, and nobody thought you would have to do all of this stuff on your own. But there is a reason for everything, and you guys are all going to do well, and there is a reason for your book. Do you do a lot of writing hun?

Me: Yes.

Catherine: Like things come up on your computer and you say, 'I don't remember writing this. I don't remember thinking that, I don't remember putting that on my computer'. But that is the way the book comes to you, Joe will help you.

You know you're meant to be writing, and this book will be about why we do Mediumship, and how it's healing.

Phone Conversation with Greg – October 2016

> *"In all the world, there is no heart for me like yours. In all the world, there is no love for you like mine." ~ Maya Angelou*

Greg and I became friends over the months after Joe's passing. He helped me many times with my grief and stress, and was a trusted confidant. The night before this informal phone reading with Greg, we were having a conversation about dating and relationships. I was not anticipating Joe coming through. During the first conversation, my phone rang and so I said goodbye to Greg. The caller did not respond to my answer and feeling a bit bad that I said goodbye so abruptly to Greg I texted him apologizing. He was also sending me a text which read: *"No problem. Funny I was in the middle of texting you when you beat me to it. You are very special and very smart. No this is not Joe talking. You deserve to be happy with someone who really appreciates you for you. Don't settle for second or third best. I really enjoyed our conversation. You're also a fantastic mom".*

I replied that I was lucky to have him as a friend and thanked him. As I sent the message to him, a Chinese message suddenly simultaneously appeared on my iphone from Greg. I copied and pasted it back to Greg and we commented that this was not the first time Joe had done this with our texts. Greg said, *"Yes, he is chatting with me now."* I told Greg to remember what Joe was saying because I wanted to hear about it the next day.

The next day I spoke to Greg to hear what Joe had been saying to him, which resulted in a very informal phone reading. Joe had not come through Greg for well over a year, but I felt Joe had some very relevant information to bring forth once again. Here is what was said in the reading:

Greg: He's rambling now.

Me: What did he say last night?

Greg: Last night he was saying how wonderful you are.

Me: When you texted me, was that coming from Joe?

Greg: No, no that was me.

Me: What else did he say?

Greg: That he would enjoy the long conversations that you guys would have together, and it would bring him much closer to you. And it was nice that you guys could talk to each other like that.

Me: Today I was cleaning some things off my dresser to put away in the special box of his stuff and I found a U2 concert ticket from 2002 on October 13. I remember walking to the concert from the parking lot in Hamilton to Copps Coliseum and I almost stepped in dog poop twice. That wasn't fun for me, but all I remember is how hard he laughed at me that rainy night. If he was here I would have taken that moment for granted, but it was actually really special because we had such fun together. We laughed so hard together and I also cried harder with him than with anyone. I was crying putting that stuff away and broke down crying in my closet. I don't know if I will ever have anything special like that again.

That's the first time I looked at the stuff from the funeral home. I looked at all the signatures in the book from the funeral home. I was amazed there were probably over 300 people there.

Greg: You both had something incredibly special.

Let me hear what he's saying,...he's saying that he feels like shit now because you're the love of his life and he always felt that way, and he realizes now that he could have handled things a lot differently, and uh…Wow, okay. He's saying he was and he still is insecure. He's saying you could have gone out with anybody.

Me: I could have gone where with anybody?

Greg: You could have dated any guy, but for some crazy, stupid reason, you chose him.

Me: That's not crazy, or stupid.

Greg: I'm just telling you what he's saying. That is just from his perspective because he knows how wonderful you are, so he's looking at it from how he was so in love with you; that he was always in love with you. Because he was so in love with you, he's looking at it from the perspective of how much you have to offer somebody, and he is saying that any guy would be crazy about you, and would love to go out with you. And the fact that you were with him! He thought if you saw his most vulnerable side that you wouldn't want to stay with him.

Me: That's crazy.

Greg: But that's where he's coming from, that's his own stuff.

Me: Wow!

Greg: What he's telling me is you never saw him at his most vulnerable because he wouldn't show that to anybody including himself.

Me: He was not vulnerable until the night before he died.

Greg: But up until then, he did a really good job of hiding it.

Me: It was hard for me to see him vulnerable, and I uh…don't know.

Greg: He wants to go back to you. The other piece to this too is, ('okay, thank you' to Joe) any guy you go out with, if they love you for you, and this is important, if they love you for you, everything else is just going to fall into place. For example, they are going to want to help you with the garden; they are going to want to help you by taking your kids to different events and stuff. It is not something you should put forward as an expectation.

Me: Right.

Greg: And they are going to want to naturally introduce you to their friends. Actually if anything you shouldn't say anything. Be silent about the whole thing and just take notes for yourself because if they're not doing any of this stuff, then these are red flags. It's not something you should bring to their attention. These are things that should flow naturally, because if someone loves you, they are going to go to the ends of the earth to help you out.

Me: Yeah but it's not even going to feel like work to them, right?

Greg: Absolutely, it won't. They are just going to naturally do. Hopefully, that will not just bring the two of you, but also your kids closer together.

Me: That's hard to imagine. I think I'm average on the outside, but I cannot imagine the male compliment of me besides Joe. My experience is very unique.

Greg: You're a very special person, Jen.

Me: Thank you. Is there anything else Joe wants to say?

Greg: He's quiet now.

Joe's messages of finding love again left me much to consider. He especially guided me into recognizing my own self-worth, with or without a partner. Recognizing our self-worth in the healing of any relationship, especially the loss of a partner is crucial to our soul experience of life on

Earth. I knew I had to get comfortable being alone on a physical plane before I could move forward and have another partner in my life. Also, having experienced such a divine soulmate relationship with Joe set the bar extremely high. What Joe lacked for me in a partner mirrored only what had been lacking in myself.

I had been failing to appreciate the value of myself and what I offered to Joe. Even after 25 years, I did not know that Joe had similar feelings of inadequacy and unworthiness in our marriage. Perhaps both of us never knew how deeply we loved and cherished each other as we were bombarded by the stressors of living an earthly life riddled with adversity. Sadly, it was only in his death that we realized the absolutely perfection of our love, a love that would continue to endure through the relationship I was beginning to develop with myself as a more evolved soul living a human existence. I had to recognize that only through living as my most actualized, higher self could I find a relationship with another that was divinely fulfilling in this incarnation.

Chapter 20

Dreams of My Beloved

"You know that place between sleep and awake; that place where you can still remember dreaming? That's where I will always love you. That's where I will be waiting." - Peter Pan

Dreams of our loved one after a sudden loss can be incredibly vivid, wonderful, sad, confusing, comforting, or even terrifying. The dreams I had of Joe have been all of these as the seasons of my grief have changed. It took months before Joe would appear to me looking as his physical self. Joe was very cautious of the ways in which he came to me in my dreams because of the disappointment of waking up struck with another realization of loss.

I spent many nights praying to Joe before falling asleep asking for him to come to me in my dreams. Many nights I missed him as much in my dreams as awake. My soul longed to connect with him but I also subconsciously did not want a dream encounter with him because of the pain of realizing the loss of Joe as a human being was tremendous. Early on, the most vivid dreams I have had of him are those in which God returned him to me and brought him back from the dead because of my faith and prayers. In these dreams, God treats me as his special child because of my devotion. I soon realized that Joe protected me in my dreams like a guardian angel.

April 2015

Just within a couple of weeks before Joe's passing, I had a very profound dream and told Joe about it as he stood in the kitchen. I told him about this vivid dream without worry as I did not fully comprehend the dream until weeks after his passing. Here is the dream:

One dark night, Joe and I were both in the water of a large lake or an ocean shore. Although not far from shore, we were in the water, holding onto small icebergs which were keeping us afloat. Behind me on my right was a large iceberg. Joe was floating on his small iceberg on my left.

Suddenly it occurred to me that the water had to be dangerously cold and that we had better swim to shore before freezing to death. In the night sky I could see the calm shore and told Joe we must swim for our life as I was afraid of the unknown below the surface.

Despite my urging, Joe refused to move and hung onto his iceberg. I told him if we did not flee to shore, we would not survive. I begged him and implored him to swim with me. I did not want to go alone. He refused and I gathered the courage to swim to shore and bravely swam up to the beach and walked on the beautiful bay in the moonlit sky.

This dream served as a powerful reminder to me about the journey of the soul and what we hold onto. Joe refused to let go of the frozen block and take the journey to shore with me. Icebergs in dreams represent the deep unknown and the subconscious mind. All we see of an iceberg is the surface, but much more lies beneath in stillness.

Regardless of what life has in store, it is important to keep swimming to shore, to keep moving. If we stay stuck in our hurt, stuck in our pain, refusing to change, there will be something greater to come and get us. We cannot ignore what is beneath the surface, deep within our souls. If we stay stuck, we'll drown in our problems. For me, the shore was a leap of faith in the night sky. I swam despite my fear of the unknown in the depth of the water. It wasn't long before I was walking on the shore and realized I was safe in a beautiful environment, but Joe was not behind me.

This dream also provided enlightenment to me that the choices that Joe and I made were our own. It was truly his decision not to keep going, no matter how much I would have begged and pleaded, he was adamant to stay back.

The shore is still and waiting, just like the peace and stillness of the universe. We are always truly safe, despite our fear of the darkness and the unknown.

June 2015

Just a few weeks after Joe died I had this amazing dream that I was sliding on the frozen surface of the lake of my childhood cottage, within a gorgeous white winter scene. I was so at peace and felt so powerful the way I could slide across the snowy white lake with such ease. This dream was a comfort and a sharp contrast to the new life I was experiencing.

Suddenly I fell underwater at the opposite barren shore of the lake. As a child, we would only canoe or boat to this side of the lake, and as a teenager, I would swim to this side of the lake without going up on the rocky shore with fallen trees. In the dream, the water was deep and I sunk down into the icy lake on my back, while seeing the surface of the opening where I fell. Joe appeared from nowhere, standing on the ice above me looking down. Without speaking, he reached his arm down to me. At that moment I knew I was safe and the dream was over. From early on after Joe's death, I knew he was protecting me in both my dreams and awake.

March 2016

Ten months after Joe's death, I had the most beautiful dream of Joe. I felt like I was surely in heaven with him.

In the beginning of this dream, I was a powerful healer. I had the gift of healing others with my hands. I was walking beside a woman of about 60 years of age with dark, short brown hair. She was complaining about her eyes and how she could not see. As I walked beside her I asked her why she thought that was. I could feel my hands getting warm and I was going to place my hands over her eyes to heal them.

Next, in the dream, I had run into an acquaintance from high school, named Eve and asked her, "How are you?"

Beloved, I Can Show You Heaven

I then dreamed that Joe had come back to life after three days because of my powerful prayers to Jesus, and I heard voices telling me that I had healed him. Joe was able to lift his casket open even with the earth on top, with the help of a young man just a few years younger than him, who he was buried beside. Coincidentally, when I woke I acknowledged that this young man was Eve's brother, Chris. Chris died a few years before and is buried right beside Joe at the cemetery.

Despite the anxiety I was experiencing in life, the next part of the dream was so heavenly. I was on vacation in the Caribbean with Joe and I could see all the beautiful resorts and pools all around me. It was one week before the kids and I were set to leave for Barbados, and Joe knew I was leaving to go away with just the kids. I was given an extra week with Joe and I felt so blessed to be there with Joe in such a heavenly spot.

The floors of the pool area had beautiful shells and sand and the water was turquoise like the ocean. It was much more beautiful than I could ever imagine. It was so nice to relax and have a week with Joe and the kids. I kept saying, "I don't know what day it is, but I have to be back at work on Monday and then I'm leaving with the kids."

I jumped in the pool and Joe was against the wall of the pool. I remember feeling the sides of his waist as I pressed against him. I remembered how I saw his cold body in the casket at the funeral, and I knew he was really healed and with me because I could feel him like he was when he was alive.

I woke up that morning feeling so peaceful like I had been on the best vacation of our lives, and I looked forward to the first vacation with the kids since Joe died. I contemplated that dream for some time in bed and immediately I drew the connection to my friend Eve at the beginning of the dream. I thought it was amazing that her younger brother Chris is buried right next to Joe on his left side. I smiled to myself and thought maybe there is some comfort between Joe and her brother knowing each other in heaven, and that in some way they helped each other out. I continued to wonder about the lady at the beginning of the dream who I assured would be healed from her blindness.

The next week the kids and I went to Barbados for March Break and we went on a tour of all the areas of the island. Barbados is divided into 11 Parishes named after Saints. St. Lucy is the only female and is situated at the very top of the island. As I heard the story of St. Lucy and how God restored her blindness from the tour guide, I was reminded of my dream only the week before. I wondered if that knowledge was the missing piece to the dream revelation. For in the dream I had been rewarded for my faith and prayers and shared a moment in heaven with my ascended loved one. But Eve and her brother Chris, who is buried next to Joe, didn't fit into the dream puzzle with the blind woman. Yet I took comfort in that part of the dream.

I recorded the dream for this book, and just over a year after that, I was in a local bookstore doing a book signing one Saturday for my first three books, when Eve walked in. Strangely, we last saw each other five years before in Sick Kids Hospital when we bumped into each other after my son's transplant. My son and I had only been at the hospital briefly that hot summer day to have his blood work done.

Eve and I embraced and she was very surprised to see me with my books. She knew of Joe's untimely death from seeing his headstone at the cemetery that was placed just six months before. She told me how sorry she was and we caught up with much to say.

Our conversation drifted to her brother and transplants because Joe had donated his kidney to our son. She told me her brother had only donated his eyes because the cancer had spread through the rest of his body. Dumbfounded I said, "Your brother donated his eyes? Wow."

"Yes", she replied, "His corneas. He wanted to donate his corneas."

I asked her if she knew who received them.

"I don't." She said.

I told her about my dream and told her that I wonder if his eyes were given to an older woman with dark hair as in my dream. "Chris and Joe are together. They 'helped each other out'. I think your brother really helped that blind person see."

Eve and I were amazed. This dream brought forth a message for both of us about our deceased loved ones in heaven. I have no doubt that Joe created this beautiful dream for me from heaven.

May 2016

One Friday night in May, about a year after Joe died I had a dream that Joe was not really dead, he had just changed his identity. He changed his identity, but the only clue I had about him was that he was driving a black Audi through the states, possibly going to Mexico. When I woke up I thought the dream was strange because I had consciously thought about the Audi car in my dream. This kind of car might be the least likely that Joe would drive because Joe worked for a different automaker.

The following evening, Hope and I watched the fireworks at the neighbours and afterward we went inside and enjoyed a cookie in our kitchen. I told her about the dream, "I had a dream that Dad wasn't dead and he had a new identity and was driving a black Audi."

Hope replied, "That reminds me of a movie where a woman steals a man's identity and he drives a black Audi."

For the life of me I couldn't think of the movie. Hope continued to give me clues, telling me that we rented it from the *Redbox*. If we rented it from there, I knew that it had to be a few years ago. I still could not remember the movie where there was a woman trying to steal a man's identity and he was driving a black Audi.

I stood still in deep concentration and repeated under my breath…a movie with an identity thief. It came to me suddenly.

"Was it with Melissa McCarthy?"

"Yes", Hope said.

"Was it called *Identity Theif*?"

"Yes," Hope continued, "We watched that movie with Dad. When we did, I asked him, what kind of car was that? He said it was an *Audi*."

I was impressed by the information that Hope had given me was so specific. Moreover, it seemed to make sense for the specific details of my dream. I was amazed and awestruck. The dream seemed so real; that Joe was trying to communicate with me. He was trying to tell me he was alive and he was trying to give me detailed to proof of this, in the dimension of the reality that I lived in, from our daughter. Something made me tell Hope the seemingly silly dream that I had about her Dad the previous night, and of all the thoughts a 9-year-old could think, she remembered a detail of a car in a movie that discussed with her father when we watched about two years previous.

My interpretation of what this dream meant is that Joe was alive and living, just in a different form, and I was trying to reach him on a physical plane. Even though Joe is in spirit, he gave me real evidence that my dreams of him were not just a product of my subconscious mind and imagination. There was evidence in this dream that was specific to Joe and the particular experience he had with our daughter in life.

June 11, 2016

Hope was at a sleepover and this was the first night that she had been away from me since Joe died. It had been a terribly busy week and I was relieved the following day was Saturday because I had accomplished so much; I was looking forward to sleeping in and taking time for myself the next day to relax.

I had been wondering why Joe didn't seem to be able to talk to me in my dreams. The common factor was that in these dreams it was too painful to accept that Joe was dead. I always sensed his spirit with me in some way, only there was a distance between us. I didn't touch, see *and* talk to him at the same time in any of these dreams.

My alarm was set late at 8:00 a.m. I continued to push 'snooze' every nine minutes being in no rush to get up. Finally sometime after 8:30, I fell into a deep twilight dream. In this dream, I was lying in bed and Joe was in the bedroom standing at the foot of our king size bed. We were looking at baby pictures of Nicholas and Faith on my iPhone (which used to be Joe's). I saw Nicholas like a tiny preemie. Then Nicholas appeared as a beautiful, healthy baby with big blue eyes and a happy smile. His face was on a gif-like image, as if you pushed a button you saw an adorable baby laughing. I noted how there was such an angelic light coming from his big baby blue eyes.

I also saw Faith as an infant of a few months old in her car seat. I noted that Faith and Hope were so much alike that I could only tell them apart from their eyes. It was fun to look at picture of our kids on the phone with Joe. I asked Joe why we didn't have pictures of Hope on the phone and then I told him my idea to purchase another cell phone and give Hope one of our old phones. I noted that made four cell phones and since there was not one for Joe, I had a sobering moment that it was because he was not with us in the physical. Then Joe told me telepathically it was a good idea to get Hope her own cell phone and the dream turned more serious.

As I was lying with my head close to the footboard, I looked up at Joe, who was then standing in my room at the window, to come to me. Next, his head was resting on his arms on the footboard as he used to do some nights as he talked to me before he was ready for bed. I touched his cheek, chin, and side of his head softly with my hands, and I could feel him as real as I ever could since his death. He felt wonderful and it was the true likeness of him, wearing his grey ribbed t-shirt.

I said to him, "Joe, I know you're dead and I am dreaming. I'm going to wake up soon, but I need to ask you: Why did you have to die?"

Joe at last replied directly to me and I waited in anticipation knowing the dream would soon be over and that I would write down what he said.

He replied in a broken sentence, "Because you are the most beautiful, and I could not bring you and the kids down with me."

There is an incredible song by Queensryche, an 80's hard rock band, entitled *"Silent Lucidity"*. This song is about the dream world where we meet our loved ones' on the other side. Our deceased loved ones do visit us often in our dreams and I know they are always watching over us. I dream of my beloved often and in many forms. It's a beautiful melody and in closing, I will leave it in these beautiful words:

If you open your mind for me
You won't rely on open eyes to see
The walls you built come tumbling down, and a new world will begin
Your dream's alive, you can be the guide but

I will be watching over you
I am gonna see it through
I will protect you in the night
I am smiling next to you in silent lucidity

Epilogue

My memories of Joe are cherished, beautiful and incredibly personal to both of us. I was more than blessed to be loved by the most incredible person to me, more than anything. And although no one could ever deny that Joe loved and adored me, no one ever saw who we were, day to day, behind closed doors without the stressors we shared.

The laughter was hysterical, the conversations deep and meaningful, his touch heavenly. Joe used to sing to me, *'Just the Way You Are'* by Bruno Mars, and told me he'd kiss me all day if only I would let him. If only I had taken up that day in the past. Now I must wait until I die and run into his arms in heaven before I can feel his embrace and kiss him all day if *he* will let me.

Though my beloved is in heaven, the sublime truth is that we are each other's heaven. As I move forward in my life without Joe in the physical, it comforts me to know that our loved ones in spirit lovingly protect and guide us.

As soul mates in an enduring relationship from a young age, Joe and I neglected to appreciate the fullness and heavenly blessings that even a life of adversity can bring. How I long for the day that Joe and I reunite as two souls in heaven and I feel his heavenly embrace.

In the time that remains of my life, it is my purpose to create a life on Earth with our children that is as close to heaven in a physical body that we can experience.

In my healing from my profound loss of my beloved, I choose to ascend. I promise my Beloved that I will take the steps in the years of my life up the stairway to heaven to be together with him again.

So you can keep me inside the pocket of your ripped jeans,
Holding me closer to `til our eyes meet
You won't ever be alone
Wait for me to come home ~ Ed Sheeran

Afterword

Just four months after my husband's death by suicide, and on World Suicide Prevention Day, it occurred to me the importance of raising awareness on suicide loss. Suicide loss is a topic that is often misunderstood in our world, especially spiritually.

My experience of suicide loss with someone so close to me and having their perspective from the spiritual, gave me a unique vantage point on this topic. I gained knowledge from having a spiritually intimate relationship with a person who died by suicide.

Although each day in the aftermath of my husband's death was a burden and a struggle, I gained tremendous comfort in knowing that we all crossover to the light and that we are all welcome in Heaven. My heart continued to ache terribly for my beloved and initially the reality of my world felt like I was awakening from the aftermath of a staunch apocalypse with a crushed heart.

I took each step in faith, looking to a future with my three children, and what I needed to create with them so we could not only survive, but thrive. The knowledge I gained about the afterlife gave me strength to carry forward, and was the catalyst for my healing.

Although arduous, there was great satisfaction in writing this book, *Beloved, I Can Show You Heaven*. As a memoir, it allowed me to express my story about my husband and our relationship through my truth and authenticity. Doing this allowed me to work through the karma I carried of being a couple with Joe for a quarter of a century, to put the past behind me, and move forward as a divine soul who is healing.

Writing this memoir also gave me the satisfaction of potentially helping others heal from loss. Love is the ultimate energetic frequency. All healing comes from love.

May you be blessed with the faith and hope that love between soulmates is eternal and never dies.

Namaste,
Jennifer

I wrote this poem just days after Joe's death. It actually came to me in the shower and I jotted it down quickly while I was in my bathrobe. I believe I channelled it from my higher self:

I am my beloved and my beloved is mine
Death cannot separate us, nor earth, nor wind, nor fire
I am all that is
I am him
He is me
The universal heart beats together in us
From creation to eternity
Love is all that is
All that is, is love

He walks with me on Earth
I love with him in heaven

He is spirit
I am hands
I wipe tears
He gives hope for the world

My beloved sees God
He is God in me.

"True love stories never have endings" -Richard Bach

References

Bill Medley and Jennifer Warnes, "(I've Had) The Time of My Life" Bill Medley, Jennifer Warnes.
   Dirty Dancing. Rec. 1987. RCA Records, Michael Llyod, CD.

Bruno Mars, "Just the Way You Are", Bruno Mars, Ari Levine, Philip Lawrence, Khalil Walton. Khari Cain.
   x. Rec.2010. CD, digital download

Dan. "Groundhog Medicine – The Wisdom of the Groundhog" *www.returnnature.us*
   June 2, 2013

Depeche Mode, "Enjoy the Silence" Depeche Mode, Martin Gore
   x. 1990. Depeche Mode, Flood. CD, Cassette

Ed Sheeran, "Photograph" Ed Sheeran, Johnny McDaid, Martin Harrington, Tom Leonard.
   x. Rec. 2014. Jeff Bhasker, Emile Haynie, CD, digital download.

"Identity Theif", 2013, Produced by Relativity Media, Scott Stuber Productions, Aggregate Films, Bluegrass Films. Universal Pictures.

Queensryche, "Silent Lucidity" Chris DeGarmo, Peter Collins
   Empire. Rec.1991. CD, Vinyl, Cassette

About the Author

Jennifer Angelee is a mother of three children and an Elementary School Teacher. Jennifer is passionate about using her unique experiences and gifts to help others who have experienced loss and life challenges.

Jennifer is trained as an Intuitive Medium, Reiki Practitioner and Angel Healer. Jennifer believes in developing our awareness of ourselves by using our life experiences to expand and evolve our souls into a greater level of consciousness.

Jennifer is also author of ***Stairway to Heaven: Simple Steps to Connect, Communicate and Find Comfort with Loved Ones in the Afterlife,*** and ***Miracles of Love, Faith and Hope,*** a mother's quest to save her son, and the medical and mystical miracles that saved him.

She is passionate about teaching children about their spiritual nature and has two children's books: ***Angel Bumps***, a story to teach children about their Soul Appointed Guardian Angel and ***I Can Show You Heaven***, a delightfully illustrated story about a child's life in heaven.

Jennifer enjoys walks in nature, writing and exploring her spirituality. During the summer, Jennifer enjoys her backyard pool and travelling with the company of her children.

To learn more about Jennifer's books and services visit
jenniferangelee.com

Manufactured by Amazon.ca
Bolton, ON